MATH
IN THE CARDS

Math in the Cards

IPMG Publishing
Johnson City, TN

www.MathGeekMama.com, a division of IPMG Publishing

ISBN 978-1-934218-02-0

MATH
IN THE CARDS

100+GAMES
TO MAKE
MATH PRACTICE
FUN!

GRADES K-8

Want to develop deep logical thinking and problem solving skills in addition to playing fun games?

Grab this free ebook to learn problem solving strategies that kids can apply to all sorts of math word problems.

Contents

Whole Number Concepts and Operations

Basic Ideas from Geometry and Measurement

Probability and Statistics

Pre-Algebra

Logical Thinking Skills

Fractions, Decimals and Percent

Interdisciplinary Games

Card Puzzles

Card Tricks

Introduction

This book is organized around common units in the K-12 math curriculum. The material is designed to serve as a reproducible resource book for teachers and parents.

Motivation, enjoyment and mastery are the main reasons for playing card games and solving puzzles. For the most part, card games and puzzles do not explicitly teach skills. However, playing, solving and creating games and puzzles can be a useful tool for diagnosis and practice. Card games provide students with an opportunity to utilize and solidify skills they have acquired. The games also provide occasions to teach skills prior to playing so that students can play well. This can reduce the number of questions such as, "When am I ever going to use this?"

Card puzzles can be used in many ways. They can be a useful supplement to regular textbook assignments. They can also be edited so that they are a part of a warm up exercise program to start a class or introduce a topic. Many teachers use the card puzzles as a part of a puzzle of the week program. The puzzles can be posted on the bulletin board or somewhere in the room for students to examine and do during some short period of time during the day or at home. The puzzles can also be done in groups or assigned as non-traditional math homework. In general, most teachers find that puzzles of the week need to be more challenging than puzzles selected as warm up exercises. Many teachers indicate that they find that posting a puzzle on Monday and then discussing solutions on Friday is an effective format. Some teachers also provide a small reward for the "most insightful or creative" solution. Others prefer to have students who correctly solve a puzzle place their name in a box and then draw for a prize.

The first section of the book provides a collection of card games. The games are group alphabetically by topic, but they are not organized sequentially.

Pages 3-67 provide whole number concepts and operations games. Some of the games, such as *Card Suit Race, Do Drop In, Horse Shoe Race, Match Up* and *Sole Survivor* provide practice with color, symbol and number recognition, counting and matching numerals. Place value, comparing and decision-making are emphasized in *Trading Places* and *Your Number Is Up*. Games, such as *Let's Predict, Make My Day Addition and Subtraction*, provide practice with basic facts. Others are addition, subtraction, multiplication and division of whole numbers games that also provide strategy formation. *Close Call, Come Closer* and *In The Gap* provide practice with estimation and mental arithmetic.

Pages 68-84 deal with basic ideas from geometry and measurement. *Build a Polygon* provides practice identifying polygons and finding perimeter. *Let It Slide, Let's Convert, Let's Estimate, Metric Ant Paths* and *One Meter Card Dash* provide experiences in metric length. The remaining games in this section are *Last Place, Creating Line Symmetry* and *Point Symmetry Rummy*. They offer concept development and practice with area and symmetry.

Pages 85-103 provide probability and statistics games. *Aces Count* and *Choosing the Best Average* are games to provide practice finding the mean, median and mode. Many statistics experts identify six steps in data analysis. They are: 1. Ask the question. 2. Collect the data. 3. Organize and display the data. 4. Summarize the data. 5. Interpret the data. 6. Make the decision. The remaining games in this collection are designed to provide students with practical examples of this process. In addition, the games *Compare and Pair, Eleven's, Getting Even, Lucky Number* and *Matched Pair* are designed to spark a discussion of gambling as a social issue.

Pages 105-113 consider pre-algebra games. *Battle It Out, Build and Take* and *Integers In Between*, are integer games involving comparing and addition. *Find the Joker* is a coordinate graphing game. *Power Play* and *Power Struggle* are working with exponents games that also involve calculator use.

Pages 114-124 move through a set of logical thinking skills games. Some of the games in this set such as *Bag It, Card Pick Up Games, Give Me a Clue, I'll Give You Some Chances, Street Hustler* and *Two Aces and a Deuce* are deductive reasoning experiences. *Yes, No, You Got It!* exposes players to the notion of a binary search strategy.

Pages 125-135 provide fractions, decimals and percent games. *Box Shot, Do You Read Me?, Decimals in Between* and *Make a Buck* are decimal games. They provide practice with place value, reading decimals and addition. *Fractions in Between* and *Two or Twenty-Two* are fraction games that examine comparing and beginning addition. *Relay The Message* is a game that provides practice finding a percent of a number and highlights women working in a non-traditional area.

Pages 136-139 provide two interdisciplinary games. *Tour the Planets* is a math and science game where the players must name the planets to earn their score. *Tour the USA* is a math and social studies game where players must name the states and capitols to earn their score.

The second section of the book provides a collection of logical thinking activities. The first part of this section provides a set of reproducible puzzles. Some of the puzzles, such as *Cards, Triangles and Patterns, Consecutive Numbers Card Puzzles* and *Border Patrol Card Puzzles*, provide practice with problem solving strategies such as finding patterns, systematic trial and error, or working backwards. Others, such as *Fancy Footwork Featuring Fours* provide an opportunity for creative practice with basic facts and order of operations. The second part of this section provides a set of mathematical card tricks.

In addition to providing many games, puzzles and tricks, this book has another emphasis-creation of new puzzles and games. Throughout the book there are suggested game variations and challenges to create new games and puzzles.

At the back of the book are teaching suggestions and selected answers.

Materials

One deck of cards for each group (Aces=1, Jacks=11, Queens=12, Kings=13).
One *Accumulation* record sheet for each player/team.
One calculator for each group.

Rules and Play

1. This is an addition, subtraction, multiplication, and division game for 2-4 players/teams.

2. The object of the game is to accumulate the highest score.

3. Play begins with the dealer placing a well-shuffled deck, face down, in a pack in the center of the playing area. Players then take turns drawing one card at a time. After each draw, players perform the indicated operation and record the result on their record sheet. For example, if a player drew a Two, and the agreed upon operation was multiplication with a current score of 6, the player would multiply 2 times 6 for a cumulative score of 12. Cards cannot be reused. In an addition game, all players/teams start with 0. In multiplication games, players/teams start with 1. In subtraction and division games, the initial score are 1000 and 1,000,000, respectively.

4. Play continues until the pack is depleted. In addition and multiplication games, the player/team with the highest final score wins. In subtraction and division games, the player/team with the lowest score wins.

Variations

- For younger players, use a smaller set of cards. Also note face cards can be removed or given a value of 10 and operations restricted.

- To make the standard game more challenging, change the rules so that the operation changes after each round and includes cards with special values. For example, round 1=addition, round 2=subtraction, etc. Special values of may be Jokers=0, One-Eyed Jacks=100, Queen of Spades=50, etc.

Round	Card	Operation	Score
1			
2			
3			
4			
5			
6			
7			
8			
9			
10			
11			
12			
13			
14			
15			
16			
17			
18			
19			
20			
21			
22			
23			
24			
25			
26			
27			
28			
29			
30			
		Final Score	

Materials

One deck of cards for each group.

Instructions

1. *Builder's Paradise* is a number sequence and counting game for 2-4 players/teams. The object of the game is to be the first player/team to use all your cards.

2. The dealer shuffles the cards and distributes all the cards among the players.

3. The game begins by having the players with Sevens line them up horizontally on the table (see below).

4. Playing in turn, each player puts down one or more cards above or below a Seven. Each card that is played must be placed vertically in the correct sequence and the same suit. For example, in the first round, sequences containing Sixes or Eights will be played.

5. If a player cannot make a play, (s)he must pass. If no cards can be played, the round ends and the player having the fewest cards wins the round and any points awarded. For example, suppose two players were playing and one player had 5 cards and one player had 8. The player with 5 cards would win the round and receive 3 points. If both players have the same number of cards, each player receives 0 points.

Variations

- Allow play both horizontally and vertically.

- For advanced play, allow diagonal placement.

Materials

One deck of cards for each group.
One *Card Suit Race* playing board for each group.
One marker for each player.

Instructions

1. This is a color recognition, counting, addition or subtraction facts game for 2-4 players or teams.

2. The object of the game is to be the first player/team to travel from start to finish.

3. Players/teams select a suit (clubs, diamonds, spades or hearts). Each player/team then places their marker on the selected starting position on the *Card Suit Race* game board.

4. Cards are shuffled and placed face down in a draw pile. Players take turns drawing one card at a time. If a player's designated suit is drawn, his/her marker is moved forward one space toward the finish. If his/her suit is not drawn, the marker stays where it is. Drawn cards are placed in a discard pile after each move. If the draw pile is exhausted before someone reaches the finish, the cards are reshuffled and players keep drawing until someone does finish.

5. The first player to cross the finish line wins.

Variations

• Make a long track by taping several copies of the appropriate sections of the game board together. Then draw two cards and move the marker forward the number value of the sum or difference of the two cards.

• Move the marker forward if the card drawn is a spade, heart or diamond and back if the card is a club. Return to start if the card is a Joker.

FINISH

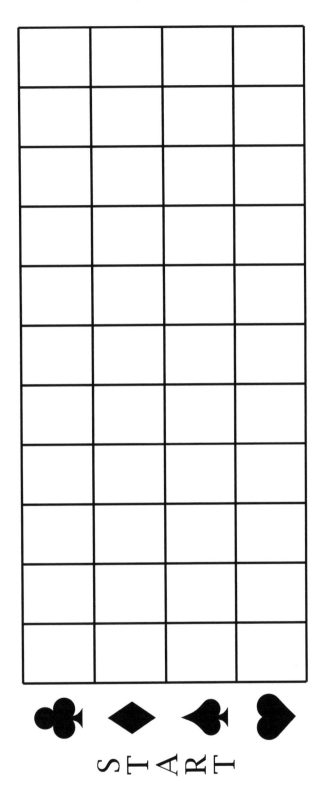

START

♣ ♦ ♠ ♥

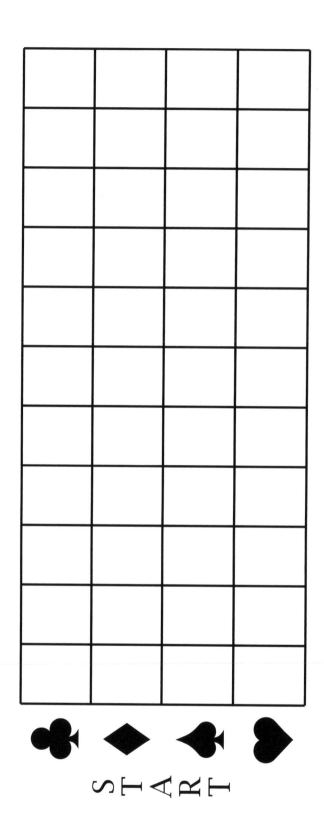

S
T
A
R
T

FINISH

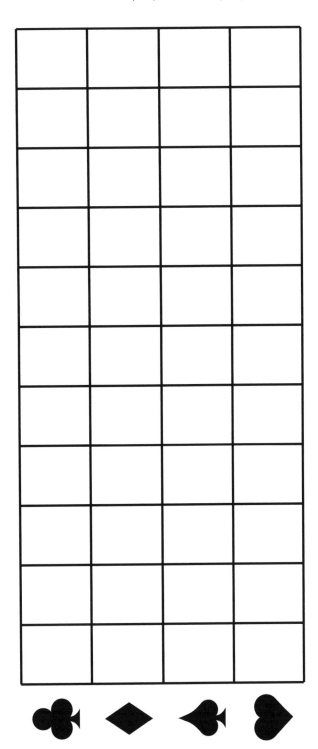

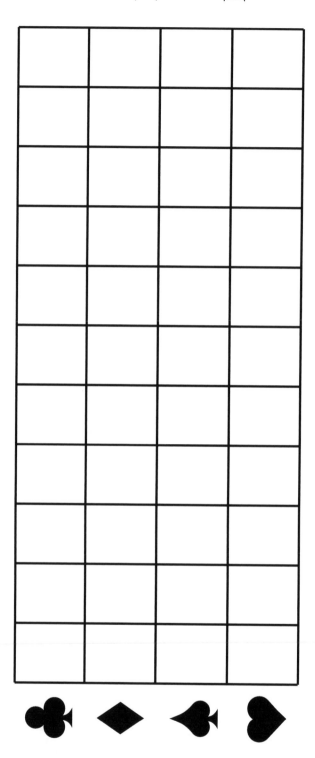

Close Call

Materials

One deck of cards for each group. Aces = 1, Jokers = 0, Tens and face cards are removed.
One *Close Call* record sheet for each player/team.

Rules and Play

1. This is a mental math game for 2-3 players/teams.

2. The object of the game is to accumulate the highest score by coming closer to the goal than your opponent(s).

3. Play begins with the dealer providing each player/team with six cards from a well-shuffled deck.

4. Players then select four of the six cards they receive and attempt to make two numbers whose sum is close to 100 without going over. Each player/team has a one-minute time limit to make a decision.

5. After the selections are made, each player puts his/her cards on the playing surface in front of him/her so that all players can see. The player/team with the total that is closest to 100 wins a point. In case of a tie, one point is awarded to each player/team. Problems, answers and scores are recorded on a record sheet at the end of each round.

6. Cards are shuffled and redealt at the end of each round.

7. Play continues until 5 rounds have been played. The player/team with the most points after 5 rounds wins the game.

Variations

- Change the number of cards dealt, used and the goal.

- For younger players, restrict the number of cards dealt to each player/team to 4, allow the use of only 2 cards, and set the goal to 10.

- To make the standard game more challenging, change the rules so that the number of cards dealt to each player/team is 8, the number of cards that may be used is 6, and the goal is 1,000. You may want to allow the use of calculators in this variation.

Close Call

Variations (continued)

- Change the scoring rules. For example, scores can be the difference a total is from the goal. If the goal is 100 and a total is 96, a player/team score would be 4. If a total was 107, the score would be 7. Scores can be totaled for all five rounds. Lowest total wins!

- Change the operation that is used. In this variation players/teams create subtraction problems where the goal is to get as close to zero as possible.

- Adjust the rules so that a player/team must come as close to the goal as possible without going over.

- Add motivational cards to the deck. For example, Jokers=0, One-eyed Jacks are wild.

Name _____

Round	Problem Created	Score
1		
2		
3		
4		
5		
6		
7		
8		
9		
10		
11		
12		
13		
14		
15		
16		
17		
18		
19		
20		
	Final Score	

Name _____

Round	Problem Created	Score
1		
2		
3		
4		
5		
6		
7		
8		
9		
10		
11		
12		
13		
14		
15		
16		
17		
18		
19		
20		
	Final Score	

Come Closer

Materials

One deck of cards for each group. Aces = 1, Jokers = 0, Tens and face cards are removed.
One *Come Closer* record sheet for each player/team.
One calculator for each group.

Rules and Play

1. This is a mental arithmetic game for 2-4 players/teams.

2. The object of the game is to accumulate the highest score.

3. Play begins with the dealer providing each player/team with five cards from a well-shuffled deck. Then the dealer turns over two or three cards. The number formed by the last two or three cards is the key number for that round. For example, if an Ace and Five are drawn, the key number is 15 or 51. The remaining cards are placed face down, in a pack in the center of the playing area.

4. Players then select three of the five cards they received. Players attempt to select three cards that when combined using any legal math maneuver, will have a result that is closest to the key number. For example, if a player draws a Five, Eight, Nine, Three and Ace and the key number was 15, then a player might select the Five, Three and Ace for play, because the product of the three numbers is 15. Players make their selections by estimating or by using mental arithmetic. Cards cannot be reused.

5. After the selections are made, each player puts his/her cards on the playing surface in front of him/her so that all players can see the cards. Each player then has the opportunity to look at the cards that the other players have selected. If a player feels that his/her result is closer to the key number than the result of any other player, (s)he stays in the game. Otherwise, a player turns his/her cards over and is out of that round.

6. At the end of each round scores are recorded. The winner of each round receives one point for having the closest result, plus one point for each player who stayed in the game. In case of a tie, the points are shared.

7. Play continues until the pack is depleted. The player/team with the highest final score wins.

Variations

- Allow the players/teams to keep three to five of the cards dealt to them.

- For younger players, restrict the combining of cards to a single operation such as addition.

- To make the standard game more challenging, change the rules so that the number of cards in the key number is 3 or 4 and increase the number of cards that must be used by each player to 4 or 5.

Come Closer

Round	Cards and Key Number	Score
1		
2		
3		
4		
5		
6		
7		
8		
9		
10		
11		
12		
13		
14		
15		
16		
17		
18		
19		
20		
21		
22		
23		
24		
25		
26		
27		
28		
29		
30		
	Final Score	

Math in the Cards
© IPMG Publishing

Materials

One deck of cards for each pair of players/teams. Aces = 1, Jacks = 11, Queens = 12, Kings = 13.
One *Cover All* game board for each player/team (see below).

Rules and Play

1. This is an addition game for two players/teams. The game begins by having the dealer shuffle the cards and place them face down in a pile.

2. Players/teams take turns drawing 1 or 2 cards. After each draw, the player/team covers the answer or numbers that total the answer. For example, if the card drawn is an Eight, a player could cover the number 8 or any combination of numbers that add up to 8. So, 1, 7, 2, 6, 3, 5 and 8 could be covered on the board. If two cards are drawn, find the sum and then cover the total and combinations that equal that total. For example, if 6 and 4 were drawn by a player (s)he could cover 2, 8; 3,7; 4,6; 9,1 because these pairs sum to 10 and 10.

3. Players/teams may pass on any turn.

4. The first player/team to cover all the numbers on his/her game board wins.

5. If the pack is exhausted before the game is won, the dealer shuffles the discards and places them face down in a pile and the game continues.

1	2	3	4	5
6	7	8	9	10
11	12	13	14	15
16	17	18	19	20
21	22	23	24	25

Materials

One deck of cards for each group. Aces = 1, Jacks = 11, Queens = 12, Kings = 13.
One *Decision Maker* record sheet for each player/team.

Rules and Play

1. This is an addition, subtraction or multiplication game for 2-5 players/teams.

2. The object of the game is to be the first player/team to reach the goal.

3. Play begins with the dealer placing a well-shuffled deck face down in a pack in the center of the playing area. Players then decide who starts and the operation to be used for the game.

4. Players take turns drawing 2 cards and computing answers. Each player may draw cards as long as they answer correctly. (S)he may stop drawing at any time. Each correct answer is added to his/her/their score for that round. If one face card is drawn or a problem is answered incorrectly, the player loses a turn and the score for that round. If a player/team elects to pass after points have been earned for that turn, the score for that round is added to the player's total. Cards are reshuffled after each turn.

5. If 2 face cards are drawn during a player's turn, points for that round and the total score are lost.

6. Cards are shuffled between players' turns. In all games, all players/teams start with a score of 0.

7. Play continues until a player/team reaches the goal. In addition games the goal is 77. In subtraction games the goal is 30. In multiplication games the goal is 368. If more than one player/team reaches the goal, the player/team with the highest score wins.

Variations

• For younger players, use a smaller set of cards. For example, use the cards Ace through 5, and the Kings and Queens, an addition goal of 47, a subtraction goal of 15, or a multiplication goal of 102.

• To make the game more challenging, create your own rules and goals. For example, spread the cards out on the playing surface and don't replenish the cards and reshuffle after each turn.

Name _____   Game _____

Operation _____   Goal _____

Draw	Cards Drawn	Running Total	Current Total
1			
2			
3			
4			
5			
6			
7			
8			
9			
10			
11			
12			
13			
14			
15			
16			
17			
18			
19			
20			
21			
22			
23			
24			
25			
26			
		Final Score	

Math in the Cards
© IPMG Publishing

MathGeekMama.com

DEFENSIVE STRUGGLE

Materials

One deck of playing cards.
One *Defensive Struggle* game board for each pair of players.
Tape two copies of page 19 together to make a 4 x 4 game board.

Rules and Play

1. This is an addition strategy game for 2 players or teams. The object of the game is to get points by forming lines of 4 cards whose sum is 10. The lines may be horizontal, vertical or diagonal.

2. Play begins by having the dealer remove the Ace through Four of each suit. Aces = 1.

3. The dealer then gives one player/team the Ace through Four of Hearts and the Ace through Four of Diamonds. The other player/team receives the Ace through Four of Clubs and Spades.

4. Players/teams take turns placing any one of their cards in any vacant space on the playing board.

5. Whenever a player/team makes a line of cards whose sum is 10, the player/team earns one point. Both players/team's cards can be used in forming sums.

6. Play continues until all the spaces on the board are filled. This is the end of a round. Keep score for each round.

7. Additional rounds are played until one player/team reaches a score of 11.

Variations

• Change the number of points required to win.

• Change the requirement to win to the best of five rounds. In this variation players/teams score one point for winning a round.

• Consider having younger players use a 3 x 3 playing board and the cards Ace through Three of each suit (sums to 6).

• For advanced play consider one or more of these options:

    a. Use a standard 4x4 board, but different sets of cards. For example, Two-Five, Three-Six, Ten-King, etc. Adjust the goal to fit the cards selected.

    b. Use the standard cards and board, but use multiplication and a goal of 24.

    c. Use a 5x5 playing board, the cards Ace through Five, and a goal of sums to 15.

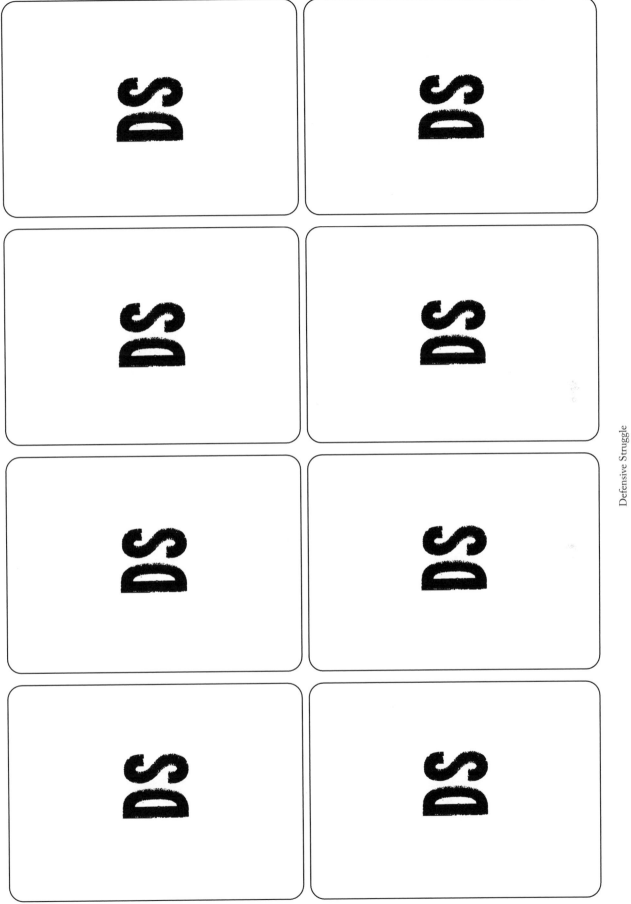

Defensive Struggle

—disclose—

Materials

One deck of cards for each group.

Rules and Play

1. This is a subtraction card game for 2 players or teams.

2. Decide who goes first.

3. Each player/team receives 2 cards. (Jokers = 0, Aces = 1, Jacks = 11, Queens = 12 and Kings = 13).

4. At the signal "go" the players/teams simultaneously disclose 1 of the 2 cards. If the cards match in color, player/team 1 receives a score of the positive difference of the number values of the cards. If the cards do not match, player/team 2 receives a score of the positive difference of the number values of the cards. Players/teams alternate who goes first.

5. Play continues until the pack is depleted. The person with the most points wins.

Variations

- Change the scoring rules so that the player/team receives a score of the sum of the number values of the cards.

- Change the scoring rules so that the player/team receives a score of the quotient of the number values of the cards.

- For younger players, adjust the rules so that only 1 point is earned each round. Do not require any computation.

- Change the rules so that the player/team who finishes with the highest score gets to spin the spinner to determine whether the high or low score will win the game. The name of this new game is *Disclose and Spin*.

—disclose—
spinner

use a pencil and a paper clip as a spinner

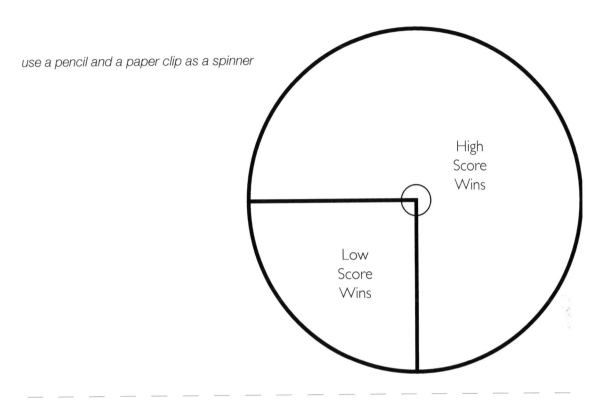

High
Score
Wins

Low
Score
Wins

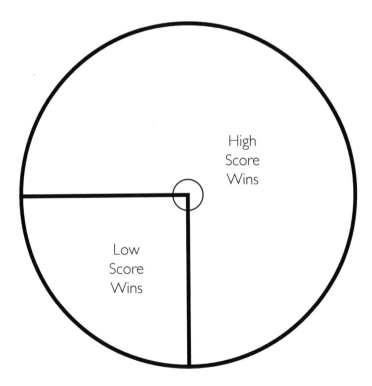

High
Score
Wins

Low
Score
Wins

Materials

One deck of cards for each group.
One *Do Drop In* playing board for each group.
One marker for each player.

Rules and Play

1. This is a counting game for 2-4 players/teams.

2. The object of the game is to be the first player/team to reach the center cell on the game board.

3. Play begins with the dealer shuffling the cards and placing all cards face down in 3 piles.

4. Next, players put their markers on the spot marked "Start" on the game board.

5. Players/teams then take turns drawing 1 card from 1 of the 3 piles and moving their marker clockwise the corresponding number of spaces. If a player/team lands on a marked space, (s)he must jump to the next inner circle. If two players/teams land on the same space, the last player/team stays and the other player/team must return to the start.

6. The first player/team to reach the center circle wins.

Variations

- For basic facts practice, allow players to draw 2 cards and then move the sum or difference of the 2 cards.

- To make the standard game more challenging, change the rules so that a player/team must travel from Start to the center of the circle and back to finish exactly on Start.

- Travel counter-clockwise.

- Change the rules so that the object of the game is to avoid the center circle. Rename the game *Elimination*.

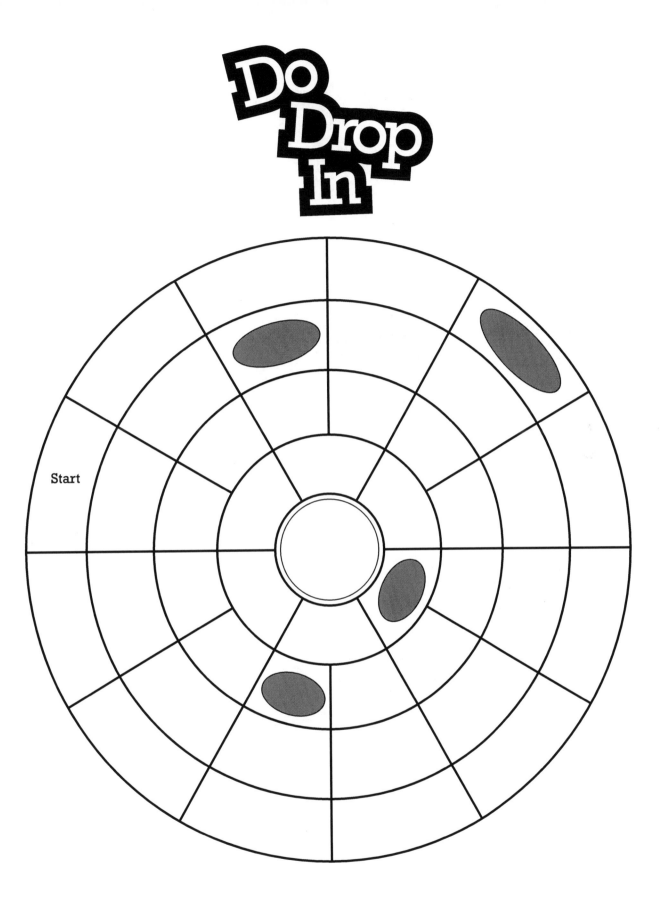

Start

Math in the Cards
© IPMG Publishing

Materials

One deck of cards for each player.
Five rubber bands for each player.
One place value mat for each player.
One ordinary die for each group.

Rules and Play

1. This is a subtraction game for 2 players or teams.

2. Bundle and set up the cards on a place value mat as shown below. Note that in this example there are 5 bundles of 10 cards in the Tens place and two cards in the Ones place.

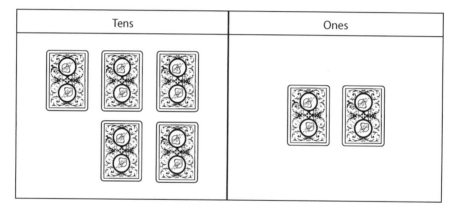

Tens	Ones

3. The object of the game is to remove all of the cards from the place value mat by rolling a die and then subtracting cards from the Ones place.

4. Players alternated turns rolling the dice. After each roll of the die, the number of cards specified on the die are removed from their board. There are two important rules:

    a. Cards may only be removed from the Ones place.

    b. If an insufficient number of cards are present in the Ones place, you may borrow a bundle from the Tens place. When you borrow a bundle from the Tens place, remove the rubber band and place all of the cards in the Ones place.

5. The game ends when no cards remain on one of the player's place value mat. The first player/team to clear their mat is the winner.

Variations

- Change the starting collection or goal.

- Use 2 ordinary dice or customized dice.

- Play the game cooperatively.

- Play the game in competitive groups. The player/team that requires the smallest number of rolls to clear the mat, within a specific time limit, is the winner.

Materials

One deck of playing cards for each group.

Rules and Play

1. This is a comparing whole numbers game for 2 players/teams.

2. Use the cards Ace through Nine of each suit and the Jokers. Jokers = 0, Aces = 1.

3. The object of the game is to earn the most points.

4. The dealer shuffles the cards and lays out 9 cards, face down, for each player at the center of the playing area as shown. The remaining cards are placed face down in a pack.

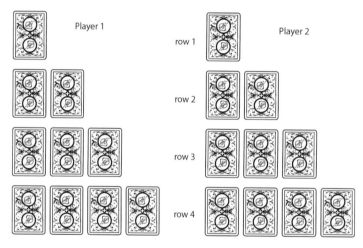

5. Play begins by each person turning over the card in the first row of his/her set of cards. Next, values are compared, and the person with the largest number value wins 1 point. If both values are the same, each player earns a point.

6. Next, the two cards in row 2 are turned over. If player 1 turned over a 5 and a 3 and player 2 turned over a 7 and a 2, then player 2 would earn two points because 72 is greater than 53.

7. Play continues until all the cards are turned over. The person with the largest number value in row 3 earns three points and the person with the largest number value in row 4 earns four points.

8. When all four rows have been turned over and compared, that is the end of the round. Record the results. If one person has reached the goal (25), (s)he is the winner of the game. If not, the cards are shuffled and redealt.

Variations

- Increase the number of players to 3 or 4. Provide each player with the Ace through Nine of a suit. Have each player shuffle and lay out his/her cards.

- Provide each of 2 players with 2 suits containing the Ace through Nine.

- Change the goal. For example, play from 0 to 50 using addition, or from 100 to 0 using subtraction.

- Change the rules so that the player with the smallest number value formed on each line wins the point or points.

Materials

One deck of cards for each group.
One *Horseshoe Race* playing board for each group.
One marker for each player.

Rules and Play

1. This is a counting and probability game for 2 players or teams.

2. The object of the game is to be the first player/team to travel from start to finish.

3. Players/teams select a color, (red for Diamonds and Hearts, black for Clubs and Spades). Each player/team then places their marker on the selected starting position on the *Horseshoe Race* game board.

4. Cards are shuffled and placed face down in a draw pile. Players take turns drawing 1 card at a time. If a player's designated color is drawn, his/her marker is moved forward 1 space toward the finish. If his/her color is not drawn, the marker stays where it is. If the draw pile is exhausted before someone reaches the finish, the cards are reshuffled and players keep drawing until someone does finish.

5. The first player to cross the finish line wins.

Variations

- *One Lane Horseshoe Race.* This game is very similar except that players race in one lane using the game board. Both players may occupy the same cell.

- *Send 'Em Back Horseshoe Race.* This game is very similar to *One Lane Horseshoe Race.* The difference is that if both players land on the same cell during the race, the player who arrives last stays and his/her opponent must return to Start.

- *+,-,x Horseshoe Race.* This game is similar to the standard *Horseshoe Race*, except players draw 2 cards and must name the sum, difference, or product. If his/her answer is correct, (s)he may move forward one space. If his/her answer is incorrect, the marker stays where it is.

Horseshoe Race

Red Black

Start   **Finish**

Materials

One deck of cards for each group.
One calculator for each player/team (optional).

Rules and Play

1. This is a game for 2-3 players or teams. The object of the game is to win points by forming the largest sum.

2. The game is played using 2 Jokers and the Ace through Nine of each suit. Face cards are removed. Jokers = 0.

3. The game begins by having the dealer shuffle the cards. (S)he then gives each player/team 6 cards.

4. Players/teams have a limit of one minute to make a 3-digit plus 3-digit addition problem using the 6 cards. An example is shown.

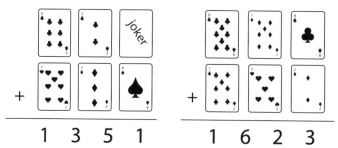

5. The player/team with the greatest sum wins the round and earns one point. The first player/team to earn 10 points wins the game.

Variations

- For younger players, deal 2 or 4 cards and form 1 or 2-digit sums.

- Adjust or remove the time limit.

- Change the scoring so that the player/team earns the number of points shown by the answer to each round. Change the name of the game to *Think Big!*

- To provide a subtraction experience, change the operation allowed to subtraction and change the name of the game to *Small is Beautiful*.

- To encourage calculator use, have players/teams form sums using more than 6 cards. Another possibility is to change the operation to multiplication or division.

Materials

One deck of playing cards for each group.
One calculator for each group.
One *In The Gap* record sheet for each player/team.
One 2-minute timer (small hour glass) or other timing device.

Rules and Play

1. This is a multiplication of whole numbers estimation game for 2 players/teams.

2. Use only the cards Ace through Nine of each suit. The object of the game is to get the highest score by accumulating the most points.

3. The dealer shuffles the cards and distributes 6 cards, face up, at the center of the playing area. The remaining cards are placed face down in a pack.

4. Players take turns trying to use some or all of the cards to make a product that is between 350 and 500. Players may use cards to make 2-digit numbers. For example, using the 5 and 8 to make 58.

5. Players have 2 minutes to create one or more multiplication problems with an answer that is in the interval. Calculator use is allowed. Players who complete the task within the time limit receive 1 point for each correct problem and answer. For example, if a player was dealt 1,5,1,6,6,8 and s(he) created the solutions 51 x 8= 408 and 51 x 8= 488, (s)he would receive 2 points.

6. A player/team may pass on any turn. At the end of each turn, the 6 cards are placed in a discard pile and a new set of 6 cards is provided from the pack for the next player.

7. Play continues until no cards remain in the pack or time is called. The player/team with the most points wins.

Variations

• Change the scoring so players receive the sum of their actual answers on a round.

• Change the goal to a different interval. For example, 700 – 1000, 2000 – 2500, etc.

• Change the number of cards in the initial deck. For example, Ace – Six, Ace – Seven, etc.

• Change the number of cards that are initially dealt. For example, deal 5 cards.

• Change the operation that is used to addition, subtraction or division.

• For older students, allow the use of exponents.

Name_____

Round	Score
1	
2	
3	
4	
5	
6	
7	
8	
9	
10	

Final Score	

Name_____

Round	Score
1	
2	
3	
4	
5	
6	
7	
8	
9	
10	

Final Score	

Name_____

Round	Score
1	
2	
3	
4	
5	
6	
7	
8	
9	
10	

Final Score	

Name_____

Round	Score
1	
2	
3	
4	
5	
6	
7	
8	
9	
10	

Final Score	

Name_____

Round	Score
1	
2	
3	
4	
5	
6	
7	
8	
9	
10	

Final Score	

Name_____

Round	Score
1	
2	
3	
4	
5	
6	
7	
8	
9	
10	

Final Score	

LAST DRAW

Materials

One deck of playing cards for each group.

Rules and Play

1. This is a strategy game for 2 players/teams.

2. The object of the game is to avoid taking the last card.

3. Play begins with the dealer placing 16 cards, face down in an array in center of the playing area (see below).

4. Players/teams take turns removing one or more cards from any row or column. Cards that are removed must be adjoining with no gaps between them.

5. The player/team who draws the last card loses.

Variations

- For younger players, play the game with a 3x3 array of cards.

- For a more challenging game, play and analyze the game with a 5x5, 6x6, or 7x7 array.

- Change the rules so that the winner is the player who takes the last card.

Materials

One deck of playing cards for each group. Aces = 1, Jokers, Tens and face cards removed.
One *Leftovers* game board for each group.
One marker for each player.

Rules and Play

1. This is a division of whole numbers game for 2-4 players/teams.

2. Use the cards ace through nine of each suit. Aces = 1.

3. The object of the game is to be the first player/team to travel from start to home.

4. The dealer shuffles the cards and lays them face down in a pack.

5. Play begins by the first player drawing 1 card from the top of the pack. (S)he then divides the number in the first cell of the board (34) by the number value on the card. The player must say the quotient and remainder. If (s)he is incorrect, (s)he must leave his/her marker at the current location. Drawn cards are placed in a discard pile.

6. Next, another player draws a card from the pack and repeats the same procedure. Note that 2 or more players' markers may occupy the same space.

7. Play continues until a player/team reaches the home cell. A player/team may enter the home cell if (s)he/hey have a remainder that is equal to or larger than needed. Discards are reused if necessary.

Variations

• Introduce chance cells involving a reward or penalty. For example, go ahead 2 spaces, go back 2 spaces, return to Start, etc.

• Change the rules so that if 2 players land on the same space, the last player/team stays and the other returns to the Start space.

• Include Tens and face cards in the pack. Jacks = 11, Queens = 12 and Kings = 13.

• Allow calculator use.

• Create a new game board using the generic master.

Leftovers

Start					
▶ 34	▶ 77	▶ 64	▶ 50	▶ 39	▼ 13
▶ 85	▶ 98	▶ 16	▶ 5	▼ 9	▼ 93
▲ 55	▶ 84	HOME		▼ 32	▼ 86
▲ 14	▲ 30			▼ 18	▼ 15
▲ 37	▲ 45	◀ 70	◀ 59	◀ 38	▼ 21
◀ 82	◀ 65	◀ 35	◀ 17	◀ 20	▼ 19

PACK

DISCARD

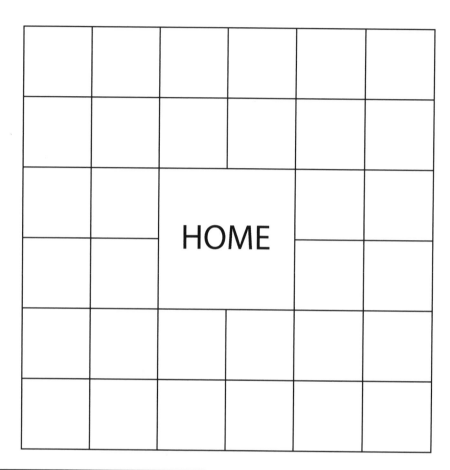

Start

HOME

PACK

DISCARD

Materials

One deck of playing cards for each group.

Rules and Play

1. This is a multiplication and probability game for 2 players/teams.

2. Use the entire deck. (Aces=1, face cards=10)

3. The object of the game is to get the highest score by accumulating the most cards.

4. The dealer shuffles the cards and distributes 5 cards to each player. The dealer also places 10 cards, face down, on the playing area as shown. The remaining cards are placed face down in a pack. The first pair of cards is turned up.

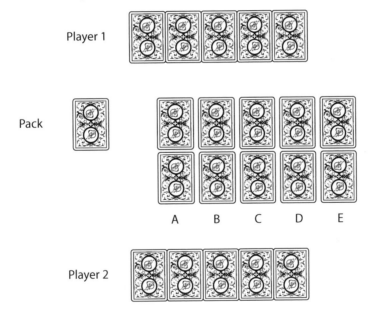

5. Players take turns turning over the 2 cards in position A and finding the product of the 2 numbers. Then they must predict whether that product will be greater or less than the product of the cards in position B. If a prediction is correct, a player may stop and remove the cards that are face up on the board or continue to guess whether the next product of the cards in position B is greater or less than the product of the next pair of cards turned over in position C, etc.

Rules and Play (continued)

6. If a player's guess is incorrect, (s)he must pay the pack the number of cards turned over on the board. The cards turned up and the cards players lose are placed at the bottom of the pack. The board is refreshed from the pack at the beginning of each turn.

7. Play continues until no cards remain in the pack, one of the player's supply of cards is depleted, or time is called. The person/team with the most cards wins.

Variations

- Play *Let's Predict* using pairs of cards and addition, with Jacks = 11, Queens = 12 and Kings = 13.

- Play *Let's Predict* using pairs of cards and subtraction, with Jacks = 11, Queens = 12 and Kings = 13.

- Play *Let's Predict* using pairs of cards and division, with Jacks = 11, Queens = 12 and Kings = 13. Calculators are recommended.

- Play *Let's Predict* using only 5 cards on the board. Predict whether the successive cards will be greater or less. Jacks = 11, Queens = 12 and Kings = 13.

- Play the original game, or variations 1-4, using the black cards as positive integers and the red cards as negative integers.

Sunday	Monday	Tuesday	Wednesday	Thurday	Friday	Saturday

Make My Day
Addition

Materials

One deck of cards for each player.

Rules and Play

1. This is an addition solitaire game.

2. Use a Joker and the cards Ace through Nine of all suits. Joker = 0, Ace = 1.

3. Deal 3 cards in the first and second rows of the array. Next, go through the pack one card at a time to try and get the correct sum by placing cards in the bottom row. Cards in the bottom row may be played in any order.

4. If you can complete the task in one pass through the deck, you win.

Challenges

Play several games. Record the number of turns needed to complete the task. Then make a bar graph of your results.

Is it possible to lose this game? Explain your answer.

Variations

• Play the game with 2-4 players. The player/team with the lowest number of turns to complete the task wins the game.

Use These Cards	Use This Mat
Ace through Nine of any suit	Basic Facts Mat
Ace through Nine of any suit	Ones and Tens Mat
Ace through Nine of any suit	Thousands Mat
Ace through Nine of any suit	Ten Thousands Mat
Ace through Nine of any suit	Hundreds Thousands Mat
Ace through Nine of any suit	Two Digit Decimals Mat
Ace through Nine of any suit	Three Digit Decimals Mat

Sunday	Monday	Tuesday	Wednesday	Thurday	Friday	Saturday

Make My Day
Addition

Use the cards Joker through Nine. Deal 3 cards in the first and second rows. Then go through the pack one card at a time to try and get the correct sum by placing cards in the bottom row. Record the number of turns needed to get the answer.

Materials

One deck of cards for each player.

Rules and Play

1. This is a subtraction solitaire game.

2. Use a Joker and the cards Ace through Nine of all suits. Joker = 0, Ace = 1.

3. Place 2 Nines and 1 Eight in the first row of the array. Then deal 3 cards in the second row of the array. Next, go through the pack one card at a time to try and get the correct difference by placing cards in the bottom row. Cards in the bottom row may be played in any order.

4. If you can complete the task in one pass through the deck, you win.

Challenges

Play several games. Record the number of turns needed to complete the task. Then make a bar graph of your results. Is it possible to lose this game? Explain your answer.

Variations

- Play the game with 2-4 players. The player/team with the lowest number of turns to complete the task wins the game.

Use These Cards	Use This Mat
Ace through Nine of any suit	Basic Facts Mat
Ace through Nine of any suit	Ones and Tens Mat
Ace through Nine of any suit	Thousands Mat
Ace through Nine of any suit	Ten Thousands Mat
Ace through Nine of any suit	Hundreds Thousands Mat
Ace through Nine of any suit	Two Digit Decimals Mat
Ace through Nine of any suit	Three Digit Decimals Mat

Make My Day
Subtraction

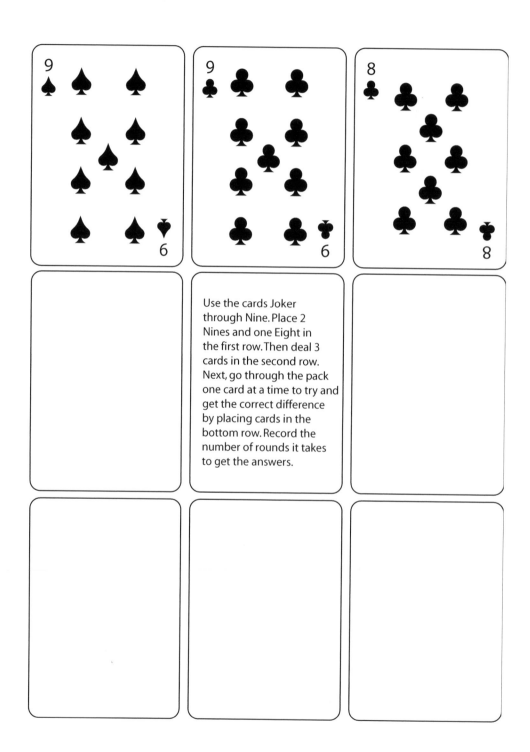

Use the cards Joker through Nine. Place 2 Nines and one Eight in the first row. Then deal 3 cards in the second row. Next, go through the pack one card at a time to try and get the correct difference by placing cards in the bottom row. Record the number of rounds it takes to get the answers.

Materials

One deck of playing cards for each group.
Match Up record sheets for each group.

Rules and Play

1. This is an ordinal numbers game for 2-3 players or teams. The object of the game is to score by matching numbers and positions.

2. Play begins by having the dealer remove the Ace through King of one suit from the deck.

3. Next, the dealer with the cards lays them face up in a line, starting with the Ace (1), in order all the way to the King (13).

4. The dealer then shuffles the cards that remain and presents the mini-deck, face down to one of the players. The cards should be displayed in the exact order in which they were dealt.

5. A "match" occurs when a card's value is the same as its position. For example, if a 3 appears third, it is a match. One point is awarded for each match. The dealer verifies and records each score for each player.

6. Play continues for 10 rounds or until time is called. The winner of the game is the player/team with the highest score. The winner becomes the dealer for the next game.

Variations

- Change the rules for winning to a goal of 100 points.

- Change the scoring rules so that players start at 100 and attempt to reach a score of zero by subtracting 1 point each time they get a match. Rename the game *Match Down*.

- Vary the placement of the cards in the initial layout. For example, left to right, right to left, top to bottom, bottom to top and require that players describe the position of the cards in terms of the initial placement. For example, a player might say, "The 3 is in the third position from the right."

Name	Round 1	Round 2	Round 3	Round 4	Round 5	Round 6	Round 7	Round 8	Round 9	Round 10	Final

Name	Round 1	Round 2	Round 3	Round 4	Round 5	Round 6	Round 7	Round 8	Round 9	Round 10	Final

Name	Round 1	Round 2	Round 3	Round 4	Round 5	Round 6	Round 7	Round 8	Round 9	Round 10	Final

Name	Round 1	Round 2	Round 3	Round 4	Round 5	Round 6	Round 7	Round 8	Round 9	Round 10	Final

Name	Round 1	Round 2	Round 3	Round 4	Round 5	Round 6	Round 7	Round 8	Round 9	Round 10	Final

Name	Round 1	Round 2	Round 3	Round 4	Round 5	Round 6	Round 7	Round 8	Round 9	Round 10	Final

Materials

One deck of cards for each player/team.

Rules and Play

1. This is a solitaire game for one player/team. In this game, Jokers = 0, Aces = 1, Jacks = 11, Queens = 12 and Kings = 13.

2. The object of the game is to discard the entire pack by removing cards from the board. The player shuffles the cards and then deals them, one at a time, face up, to the board. If the card is a Seven, it is discarded immediately. If the card is not a Seven, the player tries to find 2 or more consecutive cards on the board that have a sum of seven or a multiple of seven. If (s)he is not successful, another card is placed on the board. Three examples are shown below.

Suppose the first card drawn is a Seven of Spades. The seven is discarded and the player starts again.

Pack   Discards

Suppose the next 4 cards dealt are: Nine of Clubs, Six of Spades, Queen of Hearts and Ten of Diamonds. The Six, Queen and Ten are discarded because the sum of the values of the cards (28) is a multiple of seven.

Pack   Discards

The next card dealt to the board from the pack is placed next to the Nine of Clubs. Imagine that it was Five of Diamonds. Since the sum of the values of the 2 cards is 14, the 2 cards are discarded and play begins from scratch again.

Pack   Discards

3. Play continues until the pack is exhausted. The number of cards on the board, not including the discards, is the score for the game. Record the result.

You may modify the removal rule so that it involves a number other than 7, or multiples of 7, for a more challenging game.

Name
the
Operation

Materials

One deck of cards for each group.

Rules and Play

1. This is a name the mathematical operation game for 2-4 players/teams using one deck of cards. Aces = 1, Jacks = 11, Queens = 12, Kings = 13.

2. The game begins by providing each player with one complete suit of cards (Hearts, Spades, Diamonds or Clubs). Players take turns making up problems and providing answers.

3. Play begins by having one player/team lay out a number of cards (example: 3 cards) on the playing surface. Then (s)he must tell his/her opponent the answer (s)he obtained by combining the cards in a single operation. His/her opponent must then indicate what operation was used and how the answer was obtained within a set time limit (example: 1 minute).

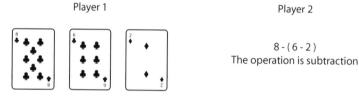

Player 1

Player 2

8 - (6 - 2)
The operation is subtraction

My answer is 4

4. Players received 3 points for giving a correct response. The object of the game is to score the most points within a time limit or specified number of rounds. For example, the first player/team to 50 wins the game. If a player gives an incorrect response, (s)he receives 0 points. If the original statement is incorrect, the opponent is awarded 4 points.

Variations

- For younger players, remove the face cards.

- Change the goal from 50 points to another goal.

- Allow the use of 2 operations to obtain an answer.

- For young players, lay out a suit of cards. Remove 1, 2, 3 or 5 cards from the suit. Have players identify the cards that are missing.

- Make the game more challenging by increasing the number of cards that can used and introducing more complex scoring.

Materials

One deck of cards for each group.
One ordinary die for each group.

Rules and Play

1. This is a multiplication facts and addition of whole numbers game for 2-3 players/teams.

2. The object of the game is to earn the highest score by drawing the most cards after a specified number of rounds (example: 10).

3. Play begins by placing the cards face down in a pack.

4. Players alternate turns rolling the die twice on each turn. The first roll tells how many piles to use. The second roll tells how many cards to place face down in each pile. The total number of cards used is the score for the round. For example, if a player/team rolled a 2 on the first die toss and a 6 on the second toss, then (s)he/they would use two piles and place six cards on each pile. Scores are recorded after each turn.

5. Play continues until seven rounds are completed. The person or team who piles on the most cards altogether in seven rounds is the winner.

Variations

- Change the number of rounds in a game.

- Change the rules for winning, e.g., the first person/team to win 5 rounds wins the game.

- Play the game cooperatively.

- Use a custom die labeled 0, 6, 7, 8, 9, 10 and two card decks to practice facts from 6-10.

Name_____

Round	Score
1	
2	
3	
4	
5	
6	
7	
8	
9	
10	

Final Score	

Name_____

Round	Score
1	
2	
3	
4	
5	
6	
7	
8	
9	
10	

Final Score	

Name_____

Round	Score
1	
2	
3	
4	
5	
6	
7	
8	
9	
10	

Final Score	

Name_____

Round	Score
1	
2	
3	
4	
5	
6	
7	
8	
9	
10	

Final Score	

Name_____

Round	Score
1	
2	
3	
4	
5	
6	
7	
8	
9	
10	

Final Score	

Name_____

Round	Score
1	
2	
3	
4	
5	
6	
7	
8	
9	
10	

Final Score	

Materials

One deck of cards for each group. Jokers = 0, Aces = 1, face cards = 10. Three targets for each group.

Rules and Play

1. This is a multiplication game for 2-3 players/teams. Lay out three sheets of papers to be used as targets, 4 feet away from the throwing area. Point values for each target are determined at the start of each game. Use the *Pitch It* score sheet and target on the following pages.

2. Players/teams take turns drawing one card from the pack and pitching the card at the targets. Each player/team throws a card from the same side. The last player/team to score throws first on the next turn. Cards are cleared from the board after each round.

3. Scoring. If:

   - A player/team draws a Five and throws it so that it touches or lands on the 3 target, (s)he/they receive 15 points.
   - A player/team draws a Seven and throws it so that it touches or lands on the 1 target, (s)he/they receive 7 points.
   - A player/team draws a Jack and throws it so that it touches or lands on the 5 target, (s)he/they receive 50 points.
   - A player/team draws a Two and throws it so that it does not touch or land on any of the targets, (s)he/they receive 0 points.

4. Scores are recorded after each round on a record sheet. The player/team to score the most points after 10 rounds wins the game.

5. If both players land on the same target, their scores cancel each other out.

Variations

- Change the rules so that the first player/team to score 200 points without going over wins the game. If a player/team goes over 200, they must start again.

- Change the values of getting a card on the targets, the number of targets, or value of the face cards. For example, targets of 10, 20, 30 and 50. Jacks = 11, Queens = 12, Kings = 13. Keep the scoring rules the same.

- Change the values of getting a card on the targets to decimals. Goals and operations can also be revised.

PITCH IT!

Name_____

Round	Score
1	
2	
3	
4	
5	
6	
7	
8	
9	
10	

Final Score	

Name_____

Round	Score
1	
2	
3	
4	
5	
6	
7	
8	
9	
10	

Final Score	

Name_____

Round	Score
1	
2	
3	
4	
5	
6	
7	
8	
9	
10	

Final Score	

Name_____

Round	Score
1	
2	
3	
4	
5	
6	
7	
8	
9	
10	

Final Score	

Name_____

Round	Score
1	
2	
3	
4	
5	
6	
7	
8	
9	
10	

Final Score	

Name_____

Round	Score
1	
2	
3	
4	
5	
6	
7	
8	
9	
10	

Final Score	

PITCH IT!

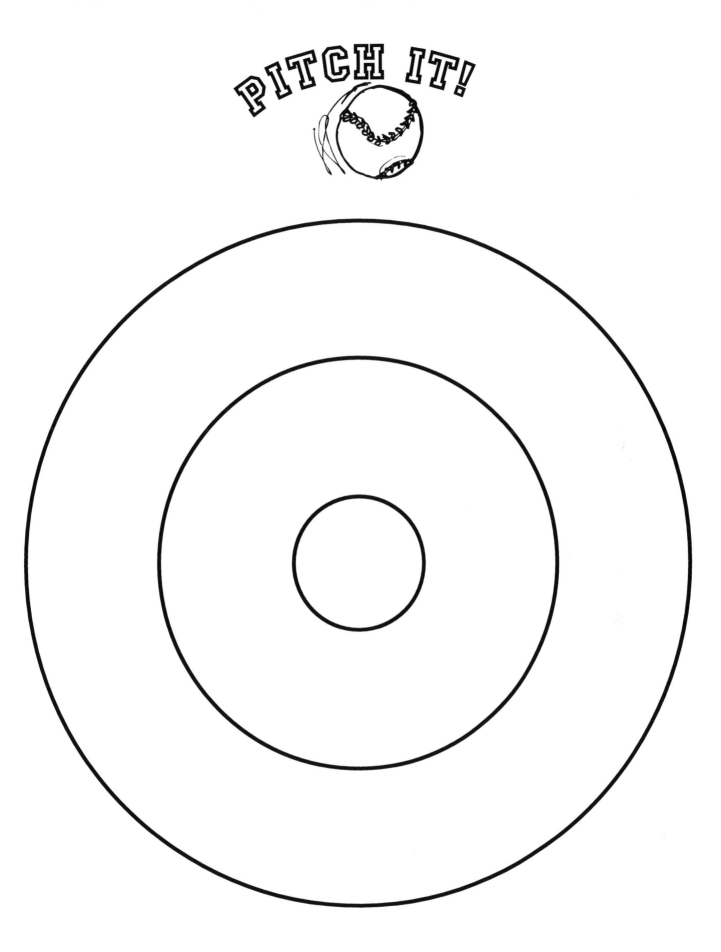

Materials

One deck of cards for each group. Aces = 1, Jokers = 0, Jacks = 11, Queens = 12, Kings = 13.

Rules and Play

1. This is a strategy game for 2 players/teams. The object of the game is to obtain the highest score by collecting cards from an array.

2. The game begins by dealing 9 cards in a 3 x 3 array as shown in the following example:

$$
\begin{array}{ccc}
5 & J & K \\
3 & 10 & 9 \\
A & 7 & 8
\end{array}
$$

3. Play begins with the first person/team selecting a card from one of the three columns. For example, the seven could be removed from the middle column. Play then passes to the next person/team. Since the seven was in the third row, one of the remaining cards in the third row must be taken. So, a player/team must select the Ace or Eight.

4. Players continue to alternate turns taking cards from a column and row until no play is possible or all the cards have been removed from the array.

5. At the end of each game or round, players/teams total the values of the cards they have collected. High total wins.

Variations

- Adjust the number of cards in the original array. For example, 4 x 4, 5 x 5, 6 x 6 or 7 x 7. Rectangle arrays can be used as well.

- For younger players, remove the face cards or make the value of each face card = 10.

- To add additional "chance" to the game, roll a die to determine who starts and the row or column that must be used.

- To make the game more challenging, make the black cards positive and the red cards negative.

- Place a mystery card or cards in the array by putting it face down.

Materials

One deck of cards for each group.
One *Quick Stop* record sheet for each group.

Rules and Play

1. This is an addition game for 2-5 players/teams.

2. The object of the game is to reach 100 without going over it.

3. The game begins with the dealer placing a well shuffled deck, face down, in the center of the playing area. Players/teams take turns drawing one card from the pack, placing it face up in front of them, and adding the value of the card drawn to his/her/their previous score. Each player/team starts a game with a score of zero.

4. Players/teams who go over 100 are out of the game.

5. The player/team who scores closest to the goal of 100 points wins the game.

Variations

- Change the value of the Joker to mean a player must start over.

- Change the scoring rules so that players must start from zero and reach a different goal.

- Change the rules so that the object is to start from 100 and reach zero by subtracting the values of the cards that are drawn.

- Change the rules so that the object is to start from 0 and reach 1,000 by multiplying the values of two cards that are drawn and adding the result to the total. Face cards = 10.

- Change the values of the cards so that the black cards represent positive integers and the red cards represent negative integers. Then change the scoring rules so that players must add the value of the card that is drawn to their score. Ace (of Spades or Clubs) = +1, Ace (of Hearts or Diamonds) = -1, etc.

- Use a mystery card or cards, such as One-Eyed Jacks. When a player/team draws a mystery card, he/she must start over.

QUICK STOP

Name ——————————————— Game ———————————————

Operation ——————————— Goal ———————————————

Draw	Cards Drawn	Running Total	Current Total
1			
2			
3			
4			
5			
6			
7			
8			
9			
10			
11			
12			
13			
14			
15			
16			
17			
18			
19			
20			
21			
22			
23			
24			
25			
26			
		Final Score	

Materials

One deck of cards for each group (Jokers = 0, Aces = 1, Jacks = 11, Queens = 12, Kings = 13).
One *Ring Your Neck* record sheet for each player/team.
One calculator for each group.

Rules and Play

1. This is a strategy game involving addition, subtraction, multiplication or division for 2 players/teams.

2. The object of the addition and multiplication games is to earn the most points.

3. Play begins with the dealer placing a well-shuffled deck, face down in a pack in the center of the playing area. The dealer then places 13 cards, face down, in a circle.

4. Players/teams take turns picking up 1 or 2 cards at a time. Play must proceed counterclockwise from the starting point to the finish. Scores are recorded after each play. In addition games, scores for a turn are the sum of the face value of any cards that are drawn. Scores are cumulative. For example, if a player selected 1 card on the first round and it was a Jack, the score for that turn would be 11 and the running score would be 11. In addition games, players/teams also receive a bonus of 50 points for taking the last card. A new set of 13 cards is dealt for each game.

5. In addition games, all players/teams start with a score of 0. In multiplication games, all players start with a score of 1. In subtraction and division games, the initial scores are 1,000 and 1,000,000, respectively. In addition and multiplication games, the player/team with the highest final score wins. In subtraction or division games, the player/team with the lowest final score wins. In all games, card values are used to add, subtract, multiply or divide the score successively.

Variations

• Change the number of cards in the circle. For example, use 21 cards.

• For younger players, use a smaller set of cards. Also note face cards can be removed or given a value of 10 or operations restricted to addition or subtraction.

Round	Cards	Round Score	Running Score
1			
2			
3			
4			
5			
6			
7			
8			
9			
10			
		Final Score	

Round	Cards	Round Score	Running Score
1			
2			
3			
4			
5			
6			
7			
8			
9			
10			
		Final Score	

Materials

One deck of cards for each set of players/teams.
One *Sole Survivor* record sheet.

Rules and Play

1. This is a number recognition game for 1-4 players/teams.

2. The object of the game is to survive.

3. The game begins by one player serving as the dealer. The dealer distributes 4 cards to each player/team from a well shuffled deck. The remaining cards are placed face down, in a pack next to the discard pile.

Pack   Discard

Player 1

Player 2

4. Next, player/team 1 must turn over the top card in the pack. If he/she has any cards matching the card that was turned over into the discard pile, he/she must put that card(s) into the discard pile. If any of the other players/teams have matching cards, they must be played as well. After all matching cards have been played, the next player/team takes a turn from the deck.

5. Play continues until one player/team has discarded all 4 cards or the pack is depleted. The player/team with the most cards at the end of the game wins. This is their score for the round. The game cannot end in a tie. For example, if both players/teams had only one Jack in their hand and Jack is drawn, the last player/team to discard the Jack wins.

Variations

• Adjust the scoring rules so that a player's score for the round is the sum of the values of the remaining cards.

SOLE SURVIVOR

Record Sheet

Name_____

Round	Score
1	
2	
3	
4	
5	
6	
7	
8	
9	
10	

Final Score	

Name_____

Round	Score
1	
2	
3	
4	
5	
6	
7	
8	
9	
10	

Final Score	

Name_____

Round	Score
1	
2	
3	
4	
5	
6	
7	
8	
9	
10	

Final Score	

Name_____

Round	Score
1	
2	
3	
4	
5	
6	
7	
8	
9	
10	

Final Score	

Name_____

Round	Score
1	
2	
3	
4	
5	
6	
7	
8	
9	
10	

Final Score	

Name_____

Round	Score
1	
2	
3	
4	
5	
6	
7	
8	
9	
10	

Final Score	

Materials

One deck of playing cards for each group.
One or two dice for each group.
Markers for each player/team.

Rules and Play

1. This is a basic facts game for 2-4 players/teams (Aces = 1, Jacks = 11, Queens = 12, Kings = 13).

2. The game begins by building a spiral board with all 52 cards. A partial setup is shown below. Note that the spiral board can be used for several games. Also note that each spiral will be different.

3. The object of the game is to be the first player/team to travel from start to finish.

4. Players/teams take turns. The roll of a die or dice determines who starts. High roll begins. The roll of a die also determines the number of spaces a player/team can move. Players then multiply the number on the die times the value of the card (s)he landed on. If the answer is correct, the player stays. If the answer is incorrect, the player does not move. If two players land on the same card, the last one stops and the other one must return to the starting position.

5. If doubles occur, such as rolling a 5 and landing on a 5, a player/team who gives a correct response may take another turn.

6. The winner is the first player/team to land exactly on the last card.

```
J  ⇒ Stop
⇧
4        8 ⇒ 10⇒ 7 ⇒ 4 ⇒ 6 ⇒ 3
⇧        ⇧                    ⇩
9        2    A ⇒ 3 ⇒ 6 ⇒ Q   K
⇧        ⇧    ⇧          ⇩     ⇩
7        J   10⇐ 6 ⇐ Start 2   A
⇧        ⇧                ⇩     ⇩
Q        9 ⇐ 5 ⇐ A ⇐ 5 ⇐ 9    7
⇧                             ⇩
7 ⇐ Q ⇐ 5 ⇐ 8 ⇐ A⇐ 6 ⇐ 3
```

Variations

- To emphasize multiplying a one-digit number times ten, change the value of all face cards to 10.

- To play a shorter game, adjust the number of cards used to build the spiral or eliminate the requirement to land exactly on the last card in order to win. To play a longer game change the "finish" to a "half way stop" so that the participants must travel from start to the half way mark and then back to start in order to win.

- For younger players consider one of these variations:

    Place all cards in the spiral face down and play with one die. Change the object of the game to simply travel the road of cards from start to finish by moving a marker the number of cards shown on each roll of the die. This will provide good counting practice and allow multi-age/ability mixing. If two players land on the same card, the last player stays, and the other player must return to start. To maintain high interest, play so that the winner must only go past finish, not land directly on the finish.

    Change the rules so that a player must name the value of the card; find the sum of the die and the card landed on, or the difference.

- Adjust the rules so that an opponent must specify what operations to use when combining the die and card.

- For more experienced players, change the value of the cards so that the black cards represent positive integers and the red cards represent negative integers.

Materials

One deck of cards for each group.

Rules and Play

1. This is a forming and reading numbers game for two players. Aces = 1, Jokers = 0, face cards are removed.

2. The object of the game is collect all the cards by forming a numeral with the largest number value using cards.

3. The game begins by providing each player with one complete suit of cards. Players take turns making up problems and providing answers.

4. Play begins by having one player deal three cards, face down, to each player and two cards, face up, to the board.

Player 1	Board	Player 2

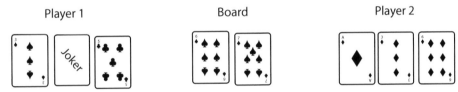

Next, players arrange their cards and the common cards on the board to form the largest whole number possible. Then, players must read the number they have formed aloud to their opponent. If a player forms the largest number and reads it correctly, (s)he wins the cards. If a player forms the largest number, but does not read it correctly, (s)he must forfeit his/her turn and place all the cards at the bottom of the pack for reuse later in the game.

5. Play continues until time is called or one player collects all the cards. The player with the most cards wins.

Variations

- For young children, lay out 2, 3, or 4 cards from the suit. Have students form 2, 3, or 4 digit numbers. In a two-card game, one card is place in the center and each player receives one card. Players try to make the largest 2-digit number. In a three-card game, one card is place in the center and each player receives two cards. Players try to make the largest 3-digit number. In a four-card game, two cards are placed in the center and each player receives two cards. Players try to make the largest 4-digit number.

- Increase the challenge by using 6 or 7 cards, 4/5 per player and 2 on board.

- Change the rules so that the player with the smallest answer wins.

- Change the rules so that the goal alternates from high to low.

- Use decimals. For example, $5.99, $92.89, etc.

Materials

One deck of cards for each pair of players/teams.

Rules and Play

1. This is an addition and probability game for 2 players/teams.

2. Players/teams take turns drawing 3 cards from the pack and tossing the cards in the air. If:

    All the cards land face up, 4 points.
    All the cards land face down, 4 points.
    Two cards land face up and one face down, 6 points.
    Two cards land face down and one face up, 6 points.

3. The first player/team to score 50 points wins the game.

Variations

- Change the scoring rules so that players earn points equal to the sum of the cards that land face up (Aces=1, Jacks=11, Queens=12, Kings=13).

- Change the value of the cards so that the black cards represent positive integers and the red cards represent negative integers. Then change the scoring rules so that players earn points equal to the sum of the cards that land face up.

Toss	Score
1	
2	
3	
4	
5	
6	
7	
8	
9	
10	
Final Score	

Toss	Score
1	
2	
3	
4	
5	
6	
7	
8	
9	
10	
Final Score	

Trading Places

Materials

One deck of cards for each group. Aces = 1, Jokers = 0, Tens and face cards are removed.
One playing mat and record sheet for each player/team.
One set of instructions for each player/team.

Preparation

Players decide if they want to play a high or low score wins the game. Labels are then added to each place value mat so that the mats reflect the number of digits and the number of decimal places to be used in the game. For example, if the game involved 5 digits and 2 decimal places, then the value place mat would be labeled as shown below.

Hundreds	Tens	Ones	Tenths	Hundreths

Rules and Play

1. This is a place value, comparing and decision making game for two players/teams.

2. The object of the game is to build the largest or smallest number.

3. Play begins with the dealer removing the necessary cards, shuffling the deck and deciding if the goal for the game is high or low score wins.

4. There are several ways to play the game.

> The first game is called *One Line Trading Places*. In this version each player/team is dealt 2-7 cards face down in a straight line. At the signal "GO," players turn over their cards and make the largest or smallest possible number using their cards. After 1 minute or when players are done, the player with the largest or smallest number wins 1 point. If the numbers are equal, both players win a point. The player with the highest score after 5 rounds wins the game.

Player 1   Player 2

Trading Places

Rules and Play

The second game is called *Square Trading Places*. In this version each player/team is dealt enough cards face down to form a 2 x 2, 3 x 3 or 4 x 4 array, e.g. 4 cards for a 2 x 2 array, 9 cards for a 3 x 3 array, 16 cards for a 4 x 4 array. At the signal "GO," players turn over their cards and make the largest or smallest number possible using their cards. Each row, column and major diagonal forms a number. Numbers must be read from left to right and top to bottom. Players must build and manage several numbers at once! After one minute or when players are done, the player with the largest or smallest number in each row, column and major diagonal wins one point. In a 2 x 2 game the maximum possible score on one round is 6. In a 3 x 3 game the maximum score is 8. In a 4 x 4 game the maximum score is 10. If the numbers formed in any row, column or major diagonal are equal, both players win a point. The player with the highest score after 5 rounds wins the game. An example of a 2 x 2 array game is shown. In this round of the game, player 1 scored two points and player 2 scored four points. Note: numbers formed horizontally are read left to right, numbers formed vertically are read top to bottom, and numbers formed diagonally are read from upper left to lower right, or lower left to upper right.

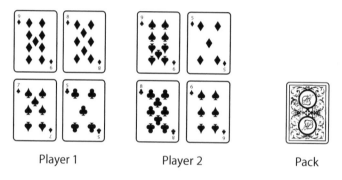

Player 1   Player 2   Pack

Variations

- For younger players, restrict the place value locations to ones and tens, or ones, tens and hundreds.

- To make the standard array game more challenging, adjust the scoring so that players must add all the numbers in the array to determine who wins one point.

- Some people enjoy making up their own *Trading Places* game using different rectangular arrays. For example, 2 x 3, 2 x 4, 2 x 5, 2 x 6, 2 x 7, 3 x 4, etc.

Trading Places

Round	Score
1	
2	
3	
4	
5	
6	
7	
8	
9	
10	
Final Score	

Round	Score
1	
2	
3	
4	
5	
6	
7	
8	
9	
10	
Final Score	

Round	Score
1	
2	
3	
4	
5	
6	
7	
8	
9	
10	
Final Score	

Round	Score
1	
2	
3	
4	
5	
6	
7	
8	
9	
10	
Final Score	

Round	Score
1	
2	
3	
4	
5	
6	
7	
8	
9	
10	
Final Score	

Round	Score
1	
2	
3	
4	
5	
6	
7	
8	
9	
10	
Final Score	

Math in the Cards
© IPMG Publishing

MathGeekMama.com

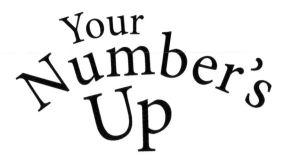

Materials

One deck of cards for each group (Aces = 1, Jokers = 0, Tens and face cards are removed).
One playing mat and record sheet for each player/team.
One set of instructions for each player/team.

Preparation

Players decide if they want to play a high or low score wins game. Labels are then added to each place value mat so that the mats reflect the number of digits and the number of decimal places to be used in the game. For example, if the game involved 5 digits and 2 decimal places, then the place value mat would be labeled as shown below.

Hundreds	Tens	Ones	Tenths	Hundreths

Rules and Play

1. This is a place value and decision making game for 1-3 players/teams.

2. The object of the game is to build the largest or smallest number. The goal is determined by the players at the beginning of each game.

3. Play begins with the dealer placing a well-shuffled deck, face down, in the center between the players.

4. On each turn, players/teams select a card and location for the value of that card on their place value mat. Players/teams must select a different place on each turn.

5. Players/teams must name the place before they are allowed to put the drawn card in that location. For example, if a player drew a Seven and the game involved 3-digit numbers with 2 decimal places, (s)he would have to say, "I'm going to put the Seven in the ones place." Locations specified must be vacant and all placement decisions are final.

6. Play continues until all places are filled. When all places are filled, the winner is declared.

Variations

- For younger players, restrict the place value locations to ones and tens, or ones, tens and hundreds.

- To make the standard game more challenging, expand the number of place value locations or play the game in other number bases. In base 5, the cards Ace through Four of each suit, plus the Jokers can be used.

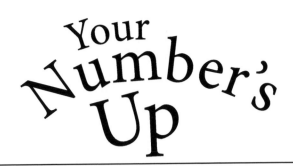

Your Number's Up

Pack

Goal: High or Low

Names	Places				

Goal: High or Low

Names	Places				

Goal: High or Low

Names	Places				

Materials

One spinner template for each group.
One deck of cards for each group.
One blank record sheet for each group.
Metric rulers (scaled in centimeters).
Compasses (optional).

Rules and Play

1. This is a card game for 2 or 3 players/teams. The game is played using a full deck. (Jokers = 0, Jacks = 11, Queens = 12, Kings = 13)

2. The object of the game is to accumulate the largest score by building polygons. Each game consists of 5 rounds.

3. Players take turns drawing cards and constructing line segments to make a polygon with 3, 4, 5, 6, 7, 8, 9, 10, or 12 sides. Polygons must fit on an 8.5" x 11" sheet of paper. For example, if a player drew a Seven, then (s)he would draw a segment 7 cm long on paper using a ruler. If a Three were drawn on the his/her next turn, then (s)he would need to draw a 3 cm segment that was attached to one of the endpoints of the 7 cm segment. After making a polygon, players must identify the shape and give the perimeter. If the answer is correct, that player receives a score of one point for the correct shape and x points, where x is the perimeter of the polygon that was constructed, for a total of x + 1 points for the round. If an answer is incorrect, the player/team receives a score of zero.

4. The winner of the game is the player/team with the largest score at the end of 5 rounds.

Variations

• Change the scoring rules so that the player/team with the low score wins.

• Change the rules so that the player/team who finishes with the highest score gets to spin the spinner to determine whether the high or low score will win the game.

use a pencil and paper clip as a spinner

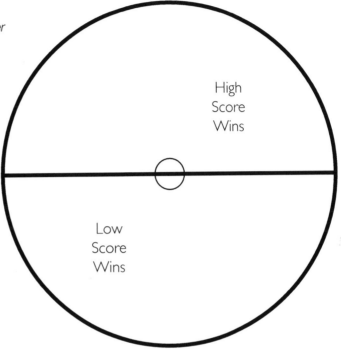

High
Score
Wins

Low
Score
Wins

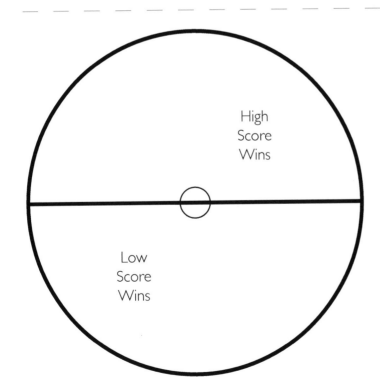

High
Score
Wins

Low
Score
Wins

Materials

One deck of cards for each player/group.

Rules and Play

1. This is a symmetry and communication card game for 2 players/teams.

2. The object of the game is to work together to copy a given arrangement of cards without peeking.

3. Each player/team starts with an equal number of cards of the same rank; 3-12 cards for each player/team is recommended.

4. Play begins by building a visual wall between players/teams.

5. The player/team who starts uses the cards to make geometric figures. Players/teams then attempt to verbally communicate how to make a copy of the figure to their teammate.

6. After a maximum of 2 minutes, players/teams compare the results. Players/teams receive one point for every card in the correct position. For example, if 3 cards were used to form a line by each player/team, then their maximum score for that round would be 6.

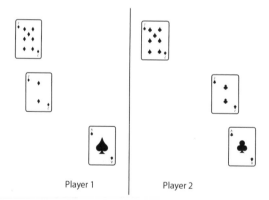

Player 1   Player 2

7. Players alternate roles after each round. The first player/team to accumulate 100 points wins.

Variations

- Change the rules so that the first player/team to win 5 rounds wins the game.

- Change the rules so that the high score within one 15 minute time limit wins.

Creating Line Symmetry

Materials

One deck of cards for each group.
One meter stick for each group.

Rules and Play

1. This is a card game for 2 players/teams.

2. The object of the game is to work together to build a symmetric figure using cards.

3. Each player/team starts with an equal number of cards; 5-10 cards are recommended.

4. Players take turns placing one card, face down on each side of the meter stick. Each time a player/team places a card on one side of the line, the partner must match it using symmetry on the opposite side of the meter stick.

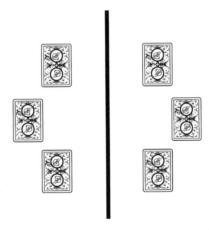

5. Points are awarded based on the number of cards used. For example, if 3 cards are used by each player/team, then the combined score for that round would be 6. Each symmetric figure built must be unique.

6. Each game consists of 5 rounds. Players/team must switch roles after each round. The player/team with the highest score after 5 rounds wins.

Variation

• Change the rules so that the first player/team to win 5 rounds wins the game.

Materials

One deck of cards for each group.
One 11" x 17" playing board for each group.

Rules and Play

1. This is an area card game for 2 players/teams.

2. The object of the game is to fill the rectangular playing board.

3. Decide who goes first. That player/team puts a card in the START position on the playing board.

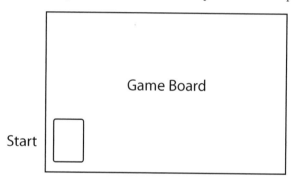

4. The next player/team puts 1 or 2 card(s) next to the first card.

5. Players take turns placing 1 or 2 cards inside the rectangle. One side of each card must touch one side of another card. Cards may not overlap.

6. The player/team who fills in the last space and names the approximate area of the board in cards wins.

Variations

• Change the size of the game board.

• Change the rules so that the board is initially completely covered and then remove 1 or 2 cards at a time. The winner is the person who removes the last card. The name of this new game is *Uncover*.

• For younger players, adjust the rules so that only one card is played at a time on each turn.

• Change the rules so that the player/team who forces an opponent to play a card outside the rectangle wins. The name of this new game is *Force Out*.

Materials

One deck of playing cards for each group.
One calculator for each person in each group.

Rules and Play

1. The game *Let's Convert* is a metric measurement conversion game for 2-4 players using one deck of cards. (Aces = 1, Jacks = 11, Queens = 12, Kings = 13)

2. The object of the game is to get the highest score by accumulating the most cards.

3. The dealer shuffles the cards and places the pack face down at the center of the playing area.

4. Play begins with the dealer turning over one card from the top of the pack. Players then try to convert that number from centimeters to millimeters.

5. The first person that can give a correct answer takes the card. If a tie results, or an error is made, the card is buried. For example: A Four was drawn. A player said "4 cm = 40 mm" and won the card.

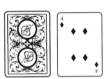

6. The winner of each round gets to draw the card for the next round.

7. Play continues until the pack is depleted or time is called. The person with the most cards wins.

Variations

Change the rules to involve other conversions within the metric system. For example:

- Convert mm to cm
- Convert cm to km or vice versa
- Convert cm to km or vice versa
- Convert m to dm or vice versa
- Convert m to km or vice versa
- Convert cl to L or vice versa
- Convert dl to L or vice versa

- Convert cm to dm or vice versa
- Convert mm to hm or vice versa
- Convert m to cm or vice versa
- Convert m to mm or vice versa
- Convert g to kg or vice versa
- Convert ml to L or vice versa
- Convert L to kl or vice versa

Materials

One deck of playing cards for each group.
One metric ruler for each group.
One *Let's Estimate* game board for each group.

Rules and Play

1. This is a metric length measurement game 2 players/teams.

2. Use the entire deck. (Aces = 1, Jacks = 11, Queens = 12, Kings = 13)

3. The object of the game is to get the highest score by accumulating the most points.

4. The dealer shuffles the cards and places the pack face down at the center of the playing area.

5. Players take turns drawing 1 card from the top of the pile. Next, the player must name a segment on the game board that is that length in centimeters. For example, if a player drew a Seven, then (s)he would need to identify a segment 7 cm in length.

6. If an error is made, the card is buried.

7. A player/team who guesses the line segment that matches the answer gets one point and records the length of that segment on the game board.

8. If a player draws a card and that segment has already been identified, (s)he loses that turn and the card is buried.

9. Play continues until no segments remain or time is called. The person/team with the most points wins.

Variations

• Identify the length of the segments in millimeters or decimeters.

• Place all cards in two piles and take turns drawing two cards, finding the sum or difference and naming a segment that has that length in centimeters, millimeters or decimeters.

• Allow the winner of the game to determine the unit of length used for the next round.

Materials

One meter stick/yardstick for each group.
One deck of cards for each group.
One graphing calculator for each group (optional).

Rules and Play

1. This is an activity for groups of 2 players/teams. The objective of the activity is to provide metric length practice. Variations include working with customary length measurement, making line graphs, reviewing mean, median and mode and inventing games.

2. Players measure 1 meter on a table and mark the length with tape. These marks are the ends of the playing field. (Two opposite edges of a table also work well.)

3. Each player/team draws 3 cards from the pack. These selections are their sliding cards. The youngest player goes first. Players/teams position themselves at opposite ends of the playing field. Players/teams take turns sliding their cards from one meter mark to the other. Players then pick their best effort, the one closest to the end of the meter stick or edge of the table, and measure the distance from the edge of the card to end of the playing field. This is their score for the round. If a card goes off the table, it cannot be used for scoring. If all 3 cards go off the table, the player receives a 100-point penalty. New sliding cards are drawn for each round.

4. Each game consists of 5-10 rounds. The number of rounds is determined at the beginning of the game. The person serving as the judge measures each attempt to the nearest centimeter. The slider records the attempt number and the result.

5. Players calculate and record their average score for the round. Play continues until the pack is exhausted or time is called. Low total for the number of rounds played wins.

Variations

- For younger players draw and slide only one card from the pack. Each player/team gets 20 tries.

- *Median Slide*. Players/teams calculate and record their median score for each round. The person/team with the lowest total wins.

- *Metric Slide*. Players/teams pick 3 cards. Face cards = 10, Aces = 1. Players' scores are the sum, difference, product or quotient of the number shown on the card "closest" to the goal and the distance in centimeters from the end line. Each game consists of 5 rounds. Low score wins.

Variations (continued)

- *Fractions Addition Slide.* Players/teams pick 3 cards. Face cards = 10, Aces = 1. Players' scores are the sum of the number shown on the card "closest" to the goal and the distance from the end line. Distances are recorded as fractions. Each game consists of 5 rounds. Low score wins.

- *Fractions Subtraction Slide.* Players/teams pick 3 cards. Face cards = 10, Aces = 1. Players' scores are the difference of the number shown on the card "closest" to the goal and the distance from the end line. Distances are recorded as fractions. Each game consists of 5 rounds. Low score wins.

- *Fractions Multiplication Slide.* Players/teams pick 3 cards. Face cards = 10, Aces = 1. Players' scores are the product of the number shown on the card "closest" to the goal and the distance from the end line. Distances are recorded as fractions. Each game consists of 5 rounds. Low score wins.

- *Decimals Addition Slide.* Players/teams pick 3 cards. Face cards = 10, Aces = 1. Players' scores for each round are the sum of the number shown on the card "closest" to the goal and the distance from the end line. Distances are recorded in tenths of a centimeter. Each game consists of 5 rounds. Low score wins.

- *Decimals Subtraction Slide.* Players/teams pick 3 cards. Face cards = 10, Aces = 1. Players' scores for each round are the difference of the number shown on the card "closest" to the goal and the distance from the end line. Distances are recorded in tenths of a centimeter. Each game consists of 5 rounds. Low score wins.

- *Decimals Multiplication Slide.* Players/teams pick 3 cards. Face cards = 10, Aces = 1. Players' scores are the product of the number shown on the card "closest" to the goal and the distance from the end line. Distances are recorded in centimeters. Each game consists of 5 rounds. Low score wins. (For practice using larger numbers, record distances in millimeters.)

- Players calculate their average score and make a bar graph picture of the results using a calculator.

- Players invent their own game based on their experience and the data they have collected.

  *All fraction games are played using a yardstick. All other games are played with a meter stick. To make any of the games more challenging, change the face card values to Jack = 11, Queen = 12 and King = 13.

Materials

One deck of playing cards for each group.
One *Metric Ant Paths* game board for each group of players.
One metric ruler scaled in millimeters and centimeters for each group.

Rules and Play

1. This is a metric measurement game for 2-4 players or teams. The object of the game is to be the first player/team to travel from nesting area to nesting area in succession. The first player/team to reach the last nesting area wins.

2. This game is played using the entire deck. Aces = 1 mm or 1 cm, Jokers = 0, Jacks = 11 mm or 11 cm, Queens = 12 mm or 12 cm, Kings = 13 mm or 13 cm. All other cards equal their face value in mm or cm.

3. The dealer shuffles the cards and places the pack face down. Players must draw one card. The player with the card representing the smallest length begins play. Players take turns in clockwise order. A play consists of drawing a card and using a ruler and pencil to draw a line segment equal to the length represented by the card in mm or cm on the game board. The first segment must be drawn from one of the ant's eggs. Each player/team makes their own path. Successive segments must begin at the end point of the last segment drawn by that player, but the next segment can be drawn in any direction on the board. Players keep their own discards.

4. Play continues until one player/team has ended a segment within each nesting spot successively. Note that a segment may not pass completely through any nesting area.

Variations

- Change the number of nesting spots required to win.

- Provide points for being the first player to reach each nesting area. The person with the most points at the end of the game wins.

- For young players use the cards Ace through Ten.

5

1

4

3

2

Math in the Cards
© IPMG Publishing

Materials

A meter stick for each group.
A deck of cards for each group.
A set of Cuisenaire rods for each group.

Rules and Play

1. This is a game for 2 players/teams. The object of the game is to be the first player to construct a train exactly 100 centimeters long.

2. To start the game, each player draws a card. The player/team with the highest card starts the play.

3. Players/teams take turns drawing a card and then selecting the rods that are the correct length. For example, if a player drew a Five, (s)he would select a yellow rod because it is 5 cm in length. The rods are placed in a straight line (like a train) along the side of the meter stick. If a player/team draws a One-eyed Jack, (s)he places a combination of rods whose total length is 11 cm and is given another turn. If a player/team draws a Joker, (s)he must remove 10 cm from his/her train.

Variations

• Change the length of the winning train (e.g. 50 cm, 2 m, etc.).

• Change the number of cards drawn.

• Play from 100 cm to 0 using subtraction.

Point Symmetry Rummy

Background

Symmetry is a kind of balance that frequently occurs in nature and in many familiar places. There are three types of symmetry.

Translation or Slide Symmetry

Slide the shape left, right, up or down without turning it and the image will coincide with the figure. In this example, the two hearts match.

Rotational or Point Symmetry

If the figure can be rotated less than 360 degrees so that it coincides with itself, the figure has rotational symmetry. In this example, the Three of Diamonds has rotational symmetry; the Five of Hearts does not.

Reflection or Line Symmetry

A figure has reflection or line symmetry if you can fold the figure along a line of supposed symmetry and the two halves of the figure coincide. In this example, the two halves of the diamond match.

Rules and Play

1. This is a point symmetry game for 2-4 players/teams using a single deck of cards. The game is played like rummy.

Point Symmetry Rummy

Rules and Play (continued)

2. The game begins with the dealer providing 5 cards face down to each player/team. The remaining cards are placed face down in the center of the playing area.

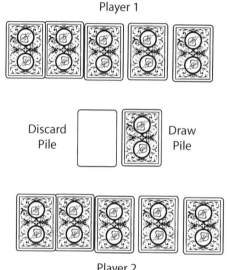

3. Play begins by the first player/team to the left of the dealer drawing a card from the top of the draw pile. This player/team must either keep the card and discard another from his hand or discard the card that was drawn. This order of drawing, deciding what to keep and discarding a card, is followed by each player/team in clockwise order.

4. The object of the game is being the first player/team to collect 5 cards with rotational symmetry.

5. Play continues until one player/team lays down all his/her/their cards and declares rotational symmetry rummy. The winner of each round earns 10 points. The first player/team to earn 100 points wins the game.

Variations

- Change the rule for a winning hand so that a player must have 5 different cards.

- Change the number of cards dealt to each player/team to 6.

- Change the scoring rules as follows: the winner gets the total of all numbers in his/her/their opponents' hands; high score at the end of 10 rounds wins.

Materials

One *Staying Above Zero* game board for each group of players.
One deck of cards for each group of players.
One marker for each player.

Rules and Play

1. This is a game for 2-4 players/teams using the entire deck. Jokers = 0, Aces = 1, all face cards = 10. The object of the game is to be the first player/team to move a marker from a starting position of normal body temperature to the boiling point of water in degrees Celsius on a metric thermometer scale.

2. The dealer shuffles the cards and places them face down in a pack on the game board.

3. Players take turns drawing a card from the pack. If the card (s)he draws is a Club or Spade, (s)he moves the temperature marker up the number indicated. If the card (s)he draws is a Heart or Diamond, (s)he moves the temperature marker down the number indicated. Used cards are placed in the discard pile. The dealer goes first.

4. If a player must move his/her marker below the freezing point of water (0 degrees Celsius), (s)he is automatically eliminated from the game. If a player lands on normal body temperature (37 degrees Celsius), (s)he may draw another card and move the amount indicated. (S)he is not required to draw a card, but if (s)he does, (s)he must move. If a player lands on the same temperature as an opponent, (s)he moves up 10 degrees.

5. If the pack is depleted before the game is finished, shuffle the discards, place them in the pack position and continue playing. If no one has won after 15 minutes of play, the player/team closest to the boiling point of water wins.

Variation

• Start from zero. Make all cards positive numbers.

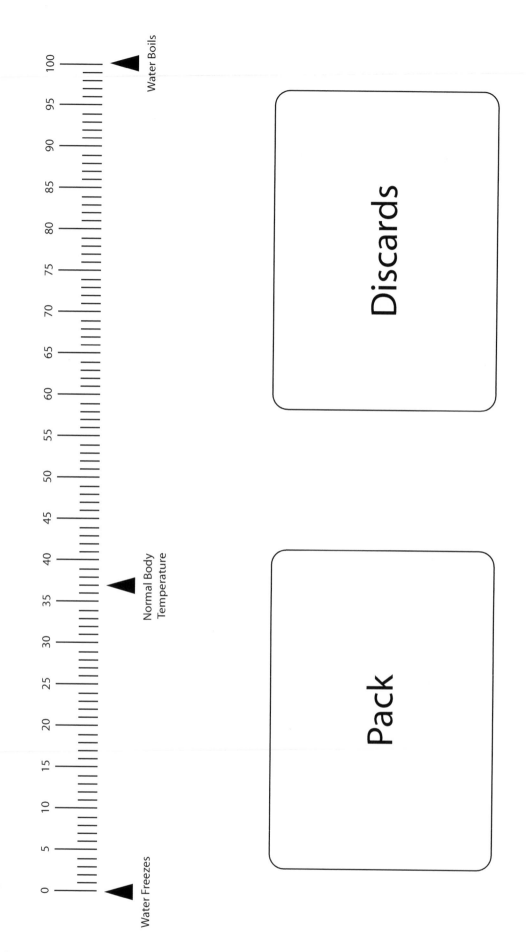

Water Boils

100
95
90
85
80
75
70
65
60
55
50
45
40 — Normal Body Temperature
35
30
25
20
15
10
5
0 — Water Freezes

Discards

Pack

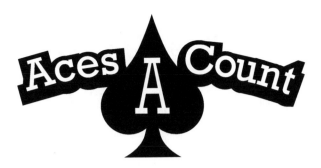

Materials

One deck of cards for each group. Ace= 1.
One record sheet for each player.

Rules and Play

1. This is a probability sampling game for 2-5 players/teams.

2. The object of the game is to score the most points.

3. In this game only the Ace through Six of the four suits are used. The reduced deck is shuffled and all cards are spread out face down on the table.

4. Each player/team draws 2 cards 3 times in a row. Only Aces count on any draw. Each Ace is worth 1 point.

5. Cards are replaced to the pack, and reshuffled after each turn.

6. The player with the highest average score after 10 rounds wins the game.

Variations

• Change the rules so that the card that "counts" is different. For example, call the game *Eights Count*.

• Change the number of cards used in the reduced deck.

Materials

One deck of playing cards for each group.
One *Choosing the Best Average* record sheets for each group.
One calculator for each group (optional).

Rules and Play

1. This is a finding averages game for 2-5 players/teams.

2. Play begins by having the dealer provide 7 cards to each player.

3. Players record the value of their cards. Jokers = 0, Aces = 1, Jacks = 11, Queens = 12 and Kings = 13.

4. Next, players/teams find the mean of their cards. Players add the value of all their cards and divide by 7.

5. The player/team with the highest average wins the round. Each round is worth one point. If a tie occurs, each player/team receives one point. Scores are kept for each round on the record sheet.

6. Play continues until all the spaces on the record sheet are filled or time is called.

Variations

- Change the scoring rules so that a player/team score is their actual average on each round and the winner is the player/team with the best average after 10 rounds.

- Change the average calculated to median.

- Change the average calculated to mode.

- Change the rules so that a player/team can choose the best of 3 averages (mean, median or mode) as their score.

- Change the rules so that each round is worth one letter in the word AVERAGE. In this variation, the first player/team to spell the entire word wins.

Choosing The Best Average

Name_____

Round	Score
1	
2	
3	
4	
5	
6	
7	
8	
9	
10	

Final Score	

Name_____

Round	Score
1	
2	
3	
4	
5	
6	
7	
8	
9	
10	

Final Score	

Name_____

Round	Score
1	
2	
3	
4	
5	
6	
7	
8	
9	
10	

Final Score	

Name_____

Round	Score
1	
2	
3	
4	
5	
6	
7	
8	
9	
10	

Final Score	

Name_____

Round	Score
1	
2	
3	
4	
5	
6	
7	
8	
9	
10	

Final Score	

Name_____

Round	Score
1	
2	
3	
4	
5	
6	
7	
8	
9	
10	

Final Score	

Math in the Cards
© IPMG Publishing

MathGeekMama.com

Materials

One deck of cards for each player/team. Aces = 1, Jacks = 11, Queens = 12, Kings = 13.
One *Compare and Pair* graph for each player/team.
One graphing calculator for each player/team.

Rules and Play

1. *Compare and Pair* is a solitaire card game for one player/team. In this game we review comparing whole numbers and pairs. We also explore how statistics can be used to analyze a game.

2. Shuffle and deal 4 cards in a line as shown below. Cards are placed face up.

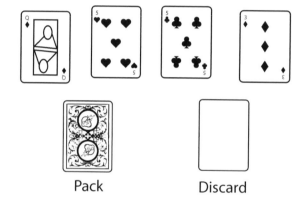

Pack   Discard

3. The object of the game is to discard all cards by pairing cards of the same rank or removing smaller cards of the same suit. In the example, the 2 Fives could be matched and then placed in the discard pile. The Three of Diamonds could also be removed because it is less than the Queen of Diamonds. After matching all possible pairs and removing all of the smallest cards of the same suit, each pile is replenished with a single card from the pack. Note that if a card is dealt on top of a matching card in a pile, it cannot be removed.

4. Play continues until all the cards are cleared or no more cards can be removed. At the end of the game, count the number of cards remaining in the piles and record the result on the *Compare and Pair* graph provided.

Exercises

1. Play several games of *Compare and Pair*. Record your results and then calculate the average score. What is the result?

2. What is the only way to remove a King?

3. Suppose the initial layout of the game contained 2 Fours and 2 Eights. Would the game be over? Explain.

4. What patterns do you notice in the results? Explain your observation(s).

5. Draw a picture of the data you collected using the histogram option of your calculator. Sketch the result. What is the range of the scores? What is the standard deviation?

6. Is it possible to win this game? If so, how often does it occur?

7. Ann said, "Fair games give each player an equal chance at winning." Is *Compare and Pair* a fair game? Explain.

8. Compare the results of the games you played using 4 cards in a line with the results of the same number of games using 5 cards in a line. Are the results the same? Explain.

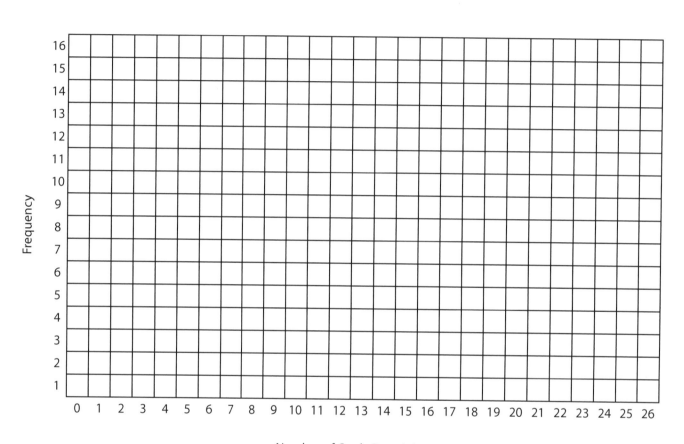

Frequency

Number of Cards Remaining

16
15
14
13
12
11
10
9
8
7
6
5
4
3
2
1

0 1 2 3 4 5 6 7 8 9 10 11 12 13 14 15 16 17 18 19 20 21 22 23 24 25 26

Math in the Cards
© IPMG Publishing

Materials

One deck of cards for each group.
One *Diamond Draw* record sheet for each group.
One sheet of square centimeter graph paper for each group.

Rules and Play

1. This is a probability game for an entire class organized in 2 player teams.

2. The object of the game is to earn the most points.

3. The game begins by one player serving as the dealer. The dealer places 2 cards from a well-shuffled deck face down on the table. Next, the player turns the cards face up. If at least one card is a Diamond, the player wins one point. If neither card is a Diamond, the dealer wins one point.

4. Play continues for ten rounds. The player/team with the most points after ten rounds wins the game and becomes the dealer for the next game.

Questions

1. Graph the results of many games. What is the probability of winning this game?

2. Is this game fair?

Variations

- Change the scoring rules so that players can specify the number of points on each round. For example, 5, 10, 20, 50, 100, 1000, etc.

- Adjust the number of rounds in a game from 10 to another number such as 100.

- Change the winning suit from Diamonds, to Clubs, Hearts or Spades.

Name_____

Round	Score
1	
2	
3	
4	
5	
6	
7	
8	
9	
10	

Final Score	

Name_____

Round	Score
1	
2	
3	
4	
5	
6	
7	
8	
9	
10	

Final Score	

Name_____

Round	Score
1	
2	
3	
4	
5	
6	
7	
8	
9	
10	

Final Score	

Name_____

Round	Score
1	
2	
3	
4	
5	
6	
7	
8	
9	
10	

Final Score	

Name_____

Round	Score
1	
2	
3	
4	
5	
6	
7	
8	
9	
10	

Final Score	

Name_____

Round	Score
1	
2	
3	
4	
5	
6	
7	
8	
9	
10	

Final Score	

Materials

One deck of cards for each player/team with the Jokers removed, Aces = 1.
Square centimeter graph paper for each player/team.
One graphing calculator for each player/team (optional).

Rules and Play

1. *Elevens* is a solitaire card game for one player/team. In this game we review sums to eleven. We also explore how statistics can be used to analyze a game.

2. Shuffle the cards. Then deal 9 cards in an array as shown below. All 9 cards are placed face up. The remaining cards are placed face down in a pack.

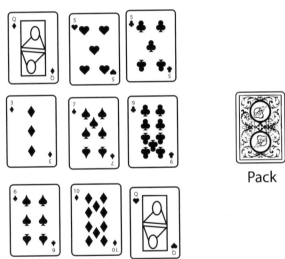

Pack

3. The object of this game is to use all the cards from the pack by playing them one at a time on the array when pairs of cards, whose sum is 11, or when face cards appear. In the example, the two queens could be covered with the first two cards from the pack. The Six of Spades and one of the Fives could also be covered because the sum of the two cards is 11. As cards from the pack are placed on the array, new combinations of 11 or face cards may appear. Cover them with new cards from the pack. Note that only two cards can be used to form a sum of 11.

4. Play continues until no more pairs of cards whose sum is 11, or face cards appear on the board. This is the end of the game. Count the number of cards remaining in the pack at the end of the each game. Record the result(s) on a graph. To win, all cards from the pack should be placed, face up, on the array and the number of cards remaining in the pack will be zero.

Exercises

1. Play at least 10 games of *Elevens*. Record your results and then calculate the average score. What is the result?

   Mean:
   Median:
   Mode:

2. Suppose the initial layout of the game contained 3 Twos and 3 Eights and 3 Tens. Would the game be over? Explain.

3. What is the worst possible score you can get in this game?

4. What patterns do you notice in the results? Explain your observations(s).

5. Draw a picture of the data you collected using the histogram option of your calculator. Sketch the result. What is the range of the scores? What is the standard deviation?

6. Is it possible to win this game? If so, how often does it occur?

7. Lynn said, "Fair games give each player an equal chance of winning." Is *Elevens* a fair game? Explain.

Materials

One deck of cards for each player/team with Jokers removed. Aces=1
One *Face Cards around the Perimeter* graph for each player/team.
One *Face Cards around the Perimeter* game board for each player/team (optional).
One graphing calculator for each player/team (optional).

Rules and Play

1. *Face Cards around the Perimeter* is a solitaire card game for one player/team. In this game we review sums to 10. We also explore how statistics can be used to analyze a game.

2. The object of the game is to place all 12 face cards in the perimeter of a 4 x 4 array. Kings must be placed in the corners or they are not counted in the final score of the game.

3. Shuffle the cards. Play begins by turning over one card from the pack. If the card is a face card, it may be placed in the perimeter, if there is a slot available. If the card is not a face card, it may be placed in any free position, including the perimeter. All 16 cards are placed face up. The remaining cards are placed face down in a pack.

4. Play continues until all 16 positions are filled with cards. Play then halts temporarily while the array is scanned for Tens or 2 cards that add up to 10. The cards that are Tens or pairs that add up to 10 are removed from the array and placed in a discard pile. Note that a card or pairs of cards whose sum is 10 can only be removed after the array has been filled. This process is then repeated.

5. The game ends when the array is filled and no Tens, pairs that add up to 10, or when a face card is drawn that cannot be played. Each player is allowed only one pass through the pack.

6. Count the number of cards that have been placed correctly in the perimeter of the array at the end of each game. Record the results on a graph. To win, all the face cards will be in the perimeter and the Kings will be in the corner. The score for a win is 12. All other scores will be from 0 to 11.

Exercises

1. Suppose the initial layout of the game contained 4 Twos, 4 Eights, 4 Jacks and 4 Tens. Would the game be over? Explain.

2. Play at least 10 games of *Face Cards around the Perimeter*. Record your results and calculate the average score.

   Mean:
   Median:
   Mode:

3. What is the worst possible score a player can get in this game? Give an example to support your answer.

4. Draw a picture of the data you collected using the histogram option of your calculator. Sketch the result. What is the range of the score? What is the standard deviation?

5. What pattern(s) do you notice in the results?

6. Is it possible to win this game? If so, how often does it occur?

7. Lynn said, "Fair games give each player an equal chance of winning." Is *Face Cards around the Perimeter* a fair game? Explain.

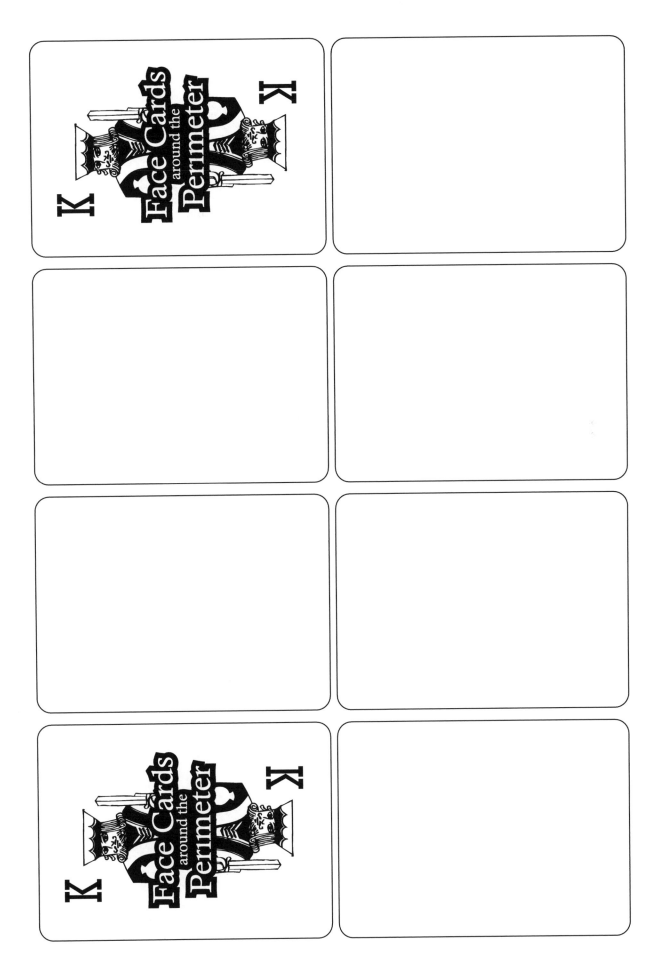

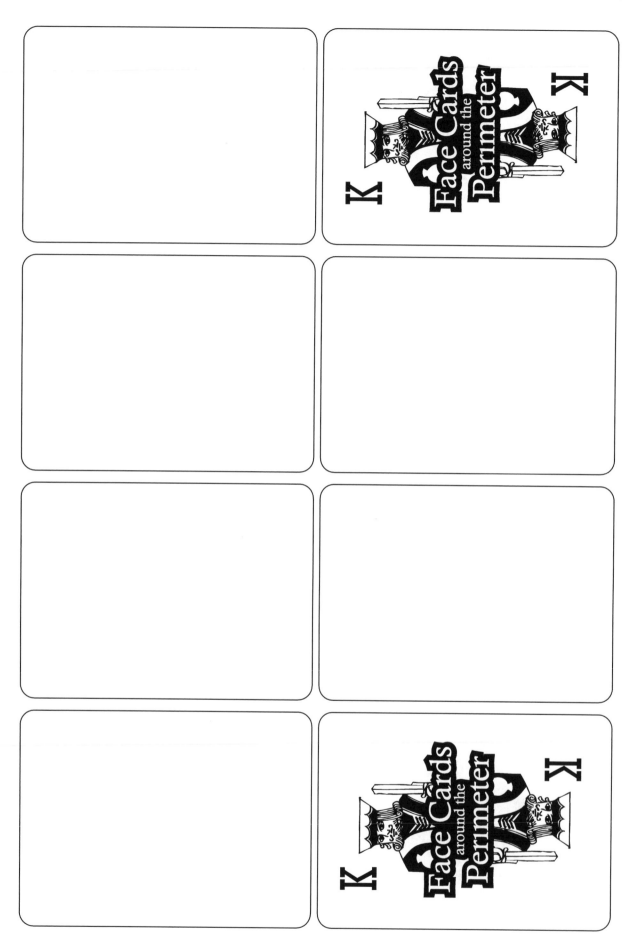

Face Cards around the Perimeter

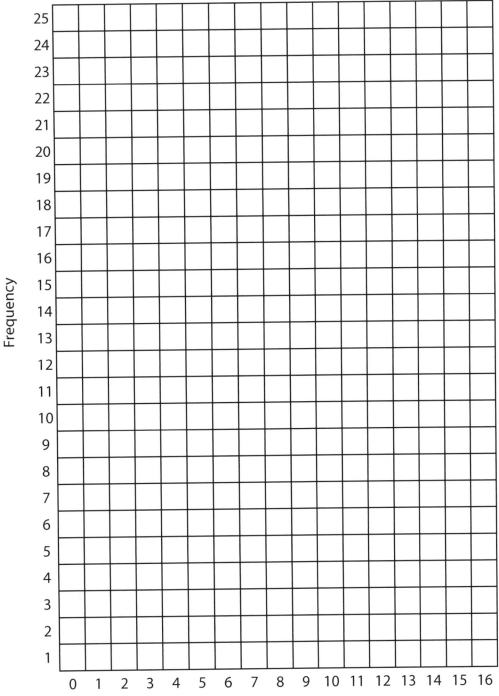

Frequency

25
24
23
22
21
20
19
18
17
16
15
14
13
12
11
10
9
8
7
6
5
4
3
2
1

0 1 2 3 4 5 6 7 8 9 10 11 12 13 14 15 16

Number of Face Cards Correctly Placed in the Array

Getting EV_{EN}

Materials

One deck of cards for each player/team (Aces=1, Jacks=11, Queens=12, Kings=13)
One piece of square centimeter graph paper for each player/team
One graphing calculator for each player/team

Rules and Play

1. Shuffle and layout all the cards in a single overlapping line as shown below. Cards are placed face up.

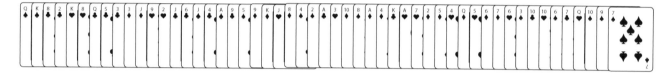

2. The object of the game is to remove all the cards from the row.

3. Adjacent cards can be removed from the row and placed in a discard pile if the sum of the 2 cards is even. For example, the Five of Hearts and the Five of Clubs could be removed because the sum is 10, and 10 is an even number.

4. Play continues until all the cards are cleared or no more cards can be removed. At the end of the game, count the number of cards remaining in the row and record the results on a bar graph.

Variations

- For younger players, remove the face cards from the pack.

- Change the removal rule to: "adjacent cards can be removed from the row and placed in a discard pile if the sum of the two cards is odd." Retitle the game as *Playing the Odds*.

- Change the record keeping so that the number of cards removed is recorded.

- Explore playing the game using other operations such as subtraction and multiplication.

Getting EV_{EN}

Questions

1. Play several games and graph the data. What is the average score? What patterns do you notice?

2. Is it possible to win this game? If so, how often does it occur?

3. Is there a strategy to improve your score or win this game? If so, explain.

Materials

One deck of cards for each player/team (Aces = 1, Jacks = 11, Queens = 12, Kings = 13).
One piece of square centimeter graph paper for each player/team.

Rules and Play

1. *Lucky Number* is a game for one player/team. In this game we review sums to 13 and explore how statistics can be used to analyze a game. The object of the game is to successfully deal and remove an entire deck from a 2 x 5 array.

2. Shuffle and deal 2 rows of 5 cards as shown.

3. Begin play by removing one or two cards at a time that sum to 13. In the example, 1 Eight and the Five, plus the Seven and Six could be removed and then placed in the discard pile. The King of Spades could also be discarded.

4. After removing all one or two-card sums of 13 from the array, cards from the pack are used to fill spaces in the 2 x 5 array.

5. Play continues. If you succeed in dealing and clearing the entire deck, you win. If not, you lose.

6. Play at least 10 games. Record whether you won or lost on the graph paper provided. When you are finished, compute how many games you won out of the total number of games played.

Variations

• Graph the total number of cards removed or the number of cards remaining in the pack at the end of each game.

• Remove the Kings from the initial deck. Change the removal rule to make sums of 12 using 1 or 2 cards. Remove the Kings and Queens from the initial deck. Change the removal rule to make sums of 11 using 1 or 2 cards. Remove the Kings, Queens and Jacks from the initial deck. Change the removal rule to make sums of 10 using one or two cards.

• Change the number of cards in the starting arrangement (e.g. 2 x 6, 2 x 4, etc.).

Materials

One deck of cards for each player/team.
One *Matched Pair* graph for each player/team.

Rules and Play

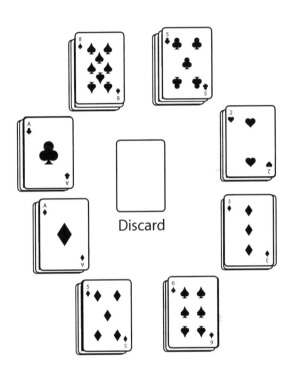

1. *Matched Pair* is a game for one player/team. In this game we review number recognition, pairing and explore how statistics can be used to analyze a game.

2. Remove the cards Nine through King from the deck. Shuffle and deal the remaining 32 cards in a circle of 8 piles with 4 cards in each pile as shown to the right. The top card of each pile is face up.

3. The object of the game is to discard all 32 cards by pairing cards of the same rank. In the example, the 2 Aces and 2 Fives could be matched and then placed in the discard pile. After matching a pair, the next card is turned up, if cards are available.

4. Play continues until the circle is cleared or no more matches can be made. At the end of the game, count the number of cards remaining in the circle and record the results on the graph provided on the next page.

Variations

- Change the initial deck so that it contains other sets of matching cards. For example, keep the Sixes through Kings.

- Decrease the number of piles in the circle, for example, 6 or 4.

- Increase the number of cards used from Ace through Eight to Ace through Nine, Ace through Ten, etc., with corresponding increases in the number of piles.

MATCHED PAIR

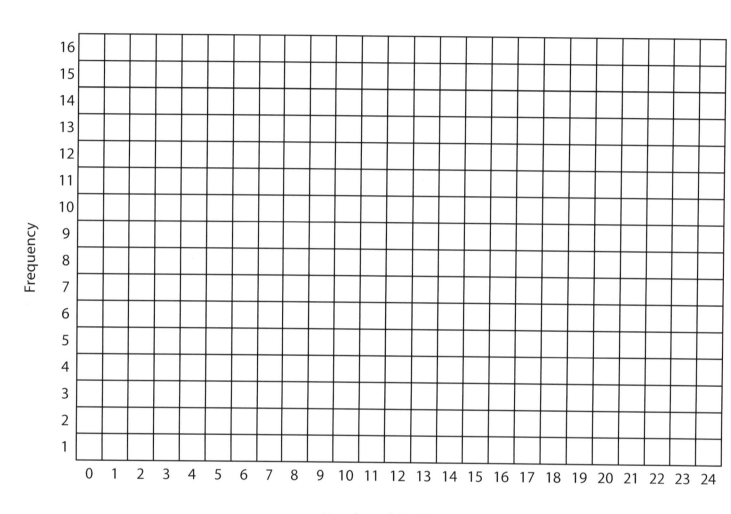

Frequency

Number of Cards Remaining

Materials

One deck of cards for each group.

Rules and Play

1. This is a comparing integers game for 2-5 players/teams. In this game the black cards represent positive integers and the red cards represent negative integers (e.g. Ace of Spades or Clubs = +1, Ace of Hearts or Diamonds = -1, etc.).

2. The object of the game is to accumulate all of the cards.

3. The deck is shuffled and all cards are dealt, one at a time, face down, to all the players/teams. Each player/team must place their cards face down on the table.

4. Play begins with players/teams simultaneously turning over one card from the top of their packs. The winner of the round is determined by who turns over the card with the highest value. The winner puts his/her winnings at the bottom of their pack.

5. In the first round, the player/team whose card had the largest numerical value takes the cards and the game continues. In the second round, the player/team with the lowest numerical value takes the cards. Each round alternates between highest and lowest values.

6. If 2 or more players/teams turn over cards with the same color and numerical value, a "battle" results. In a battle, each player/team places 2 cards face down and turns up a third card. The player/team whose third card is high or low (depending on the round) wins the battle. If another tie results, the procedure is repeated. The winner of the battle wins all the cards.

7. The winner of the game is the player/team who accumulates all of the cards. If time does not permit accumulation of all the cards, the player/team with the most cards wins.

Variations

- High card wins every round.

- Low card wins every round.

- For younger players, use only positive values for the cards.

Materials

One deck of cards for each group.

Rules and Play

1. *Build and Take* is an addition and subtraction of integers game for 2-4 players. The black cards represent positive integers and the red cards represent negative integers.

2. The object of this game is to collect the most cards.

3. The dealer supplies each player with 4 cards. Four cards are also dealt face up on the table and the remaining cards are placed face down in a pack.

Player 1

Pack

Player 2

Note: Aces= + /-1, Kings, Queens, Jacks= +/-13, +/-12, +/-11 and all other cards are face value, respectively.

4. Players take turns attempting to form sums or differences whose answer is zero. Each player attempts to remove one or more cards from the table by combining cards in his/her hand with one or more cards on the table in such a way that the answer is zero. In the example above, if player 1 had a Five of Diamonds and a Two of Clubs then (s)he could remove the Three of Diamonds from the board because -5 + +2 = -3. It is important to note that combinations of cards from a hand or the table can be used.

5. Two (2) minutes are allowed for each player to complete his/her turn.

6. After each player completes a turn, the table and that player's hand are replenished. In the unlikely event that no play is possible then that board is buried, the board is replenished and play passes to the next player.

7. Play continues until one pass through the pack is completed. The player who takes the last trick also wins the remaining cards on the table and in other players' hands.

8. The game ends when the pack is depleted, when time is called, or when no play is possible by all people in the game. The player with the most cards wins.

Variations

- Change the scoring rules.

   a. On each round award 2 points for the most cards and 2 points for Aces or one-eyed face cards. The first player to accumulate 50 points wins the game.

   b. Stop the game after one pass through the deck and then have each player total his/her entire collection. The winner is the player with the largest total.

- To make the game easier, remove the face cards.

- To make the game more challenging, change the rules so that if a Jack is used you must multiply by 2; if a Queen is used you must multiply by 4; and if a King is used you must multiply by 10.

Materials

One deck of cards for each pair of players/teams. (52 cards + 1 Joker).

Rules and Play

1. This is a graphing game for 2- 5 players/teams. The object of the game is to find the hidden Joker in as few guesses as possible.

2. The game begins by placing 49 cards face down in a 7 x 7 array. Then have one player hide the Joker in a secret spot by removing one card and placing the Joker face down in that spot. Record the location of the spot using coordinates.

3. After the Joker is hidden, players try to guess the location by specifying grid spots. The center card is (0,0). After each try, the player who hid the Joker must turn over the card at the specified location. If it is not the Joker, (s)he must tell the approximate direction to go look for the Joker using the points on a compass. If the Joker is found, the round ends and the number of turns required is recorded.

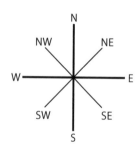

			3			
			2			
			1			
-3	-2	-1	0	1	2	3
			-1			
			-2			
			-3			

4. Players alternate roles after each round. The player who finds the Joker in the fewest turns wins the game.

Variations

- For a first quadrant experience, label the axes from 1 to 7. The coordinates for the lower left card are (1,1).

- For younger players, play a linear game where clues indicate only north, south, east or west.

- Change the number of cards in the square array (e.g. 16, 25, 36).

- Change the dimensions of the array (e.g. 13 x 4).

Integers In Between

Materials

One deck of cards for each group.

Rules and Play

1. This is a comparing integers game for 2-3 players/teams. Each black card is a positive integer and each red card is a negative integer. Jokers= 0, Aces= +/- 1, Jacks= +/- 11, Queens= +/- 12, Kings= +/- 13.

2. The object of the game is to get the most points. Players/teams earn points by predicting whether or not a card that is drawn will have a value that is between the values of 2 given cards.

3. Players/teams take turns predicting if the value of the card in the middle will be between the others. If the player/team guesses correctly, (s)he/they get one point. If not they get zero points. The player or team with the high score after one pass through the deck wins the game.

4. Play begins with the dealer providing 2 cards face up, and 1 card face down to each player. An example is shown below.

The dealer provides these cards.

The player predicted that the value of the mystery card in the middle would *not* be between the values of the other 2 cards. If the mystery card was a Six of Spades, the player's score for that round would be zero. If the mystery card was the Three of Diamonds, the player's score for the round would be 1 point.

Variations

- For younger players, make all cards positive integers. Turn all cards face up and have players tell if the card in the middle has a value between the other two. If (s)he is correct, the player gets 3 points. If the answer is correct, but the value of the card in the middle is not between the others, the player gets 2 points.

- To make the standard games more challenging, change the rules so that a player/team must get 2 or 3 cards with values between the initial pair that are drawn. For example, if a Two of Clubs and a King of Spades were drawn, then the player must draw 2 cards that have a value between 2 and 13.

Materials

One deck of cards for each group.
One calculator for each player.

Rules and Play

1. *Power Play* is an exponents card game for 2 players/teams.

2. The dealer removes all of the face cards and tens from the deck. Aces = 1, Jokers = 0.

3. The dealer places the cards face down in two piles. There should be an equal number of cards in each pile.

4. Play begins by having the dealer turn over the top card in each pile. A sample is shown below. In this example, the first player to give the correct answer (8) wins the cards. If a tie results, the top cards are placed at the bottom of each pile. If a player/team gives an incorrect answer, the opponent gets a "free" turn.

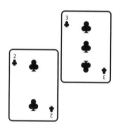

5. Play continues until the piles are depleted. The player/team with the most cards wins the game.

Variations

- Change the rules so that players/teams use a complete deck to form an expression, A$^{(B)}$ for cards A and B. Note that this change will cause most calculators to occasionally overflow and present answers in scientific notation.

- Change the rules so that the player/team who finishes with the highest score gets to spin the spinner to determine whether the high or low score will win the game. The name of this game is *Power Doesn't Always Win*.

POWER PLAY

use a pencil and paper clip as a spinner

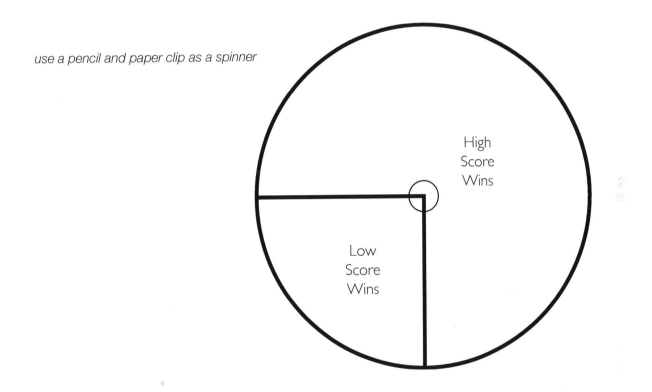

High
Score
Wins

Low
Score
Wins

Materials

One deck of cards for each player.
One *Power Struggle* record sheet for each player.
One calculator for each player.

Rules and Play

1. This is an exponents card game for two players/teams.

2. The game is played using the Ace-Four of each suit.

3. Each player/team receives 3 cards (Jokers = 0, Aces = 1). Players have one minute to manipulate the cards to create and evaluate an expression of the $(A^B)^C$. For example, if a player was dealt a Two, Three and Four, (s)he could say $(2^3)^4 = 8^4$ or 4096. In this example, 4096 would be the score for the round.

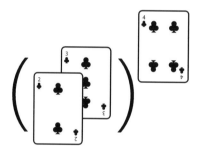

4. The object of the game is to get the highest score. Each game consists of 10 rounds.

Variations

- Change the scoring rules so that the player/team with the low score wins.

- Change the scoring rules so that player/team receives a score derived from evaluating the expression $A^{(B^C)}$ for cards A, B, and C. Note that this change will cause most calculators to express answers in scientific notation.

- Change the rules so that the player/team who finishes with the highest score gets to spin the spinner to determine whether or high or low score will win the game. The name of this new game is *Power Doesn't Always Win*.

Name_____   Name_____   Name_____

Round	Score
1	
2	
3	
4	
5	
6	
7	
8	
9	
10	

Final Score	

Round	Score
1	
2	
3	
4	
5	
6	
7	
8	
9	
10	

Final Score	

Round	Score
1	
2	
3	
4	
5	
6	
7	
8	
9	
10	

Final Score	

use a pencil and paper clip as a spinner

High
Score
Wins

Low
Score
Wins

MathGeekMama.com

Materials

One deck of cards for each group.
One paper bag for each group.

Rules and Play

1. This is a logic game for 2-4 players/teams.

2. The object of the game is to collect the most points by guessing the number of cards in a bag.

3. Play begins with the dealer selecting between 2 and 10 cards, and placing them in a bag. For example, 3 cards could be placed in a bag.

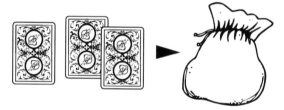

Next, the dealer tells the total number of cards in the bag and the suits, but not how many of each rank. Players/teams take turns attempting to guess the exact cards in the bag by sampling one card at a time. After a player looks at a card it must be returned to the bag. Players continue sampling one card at a time as long as they want or until they think they know how many cards of each suit and rank are in the bag.

4. If a player's guess is correct, points are awarded according to the following scheme: Score= 52 - No. of guesses. If a player's guess is incorrect, his/her score is zero.

5. Play continues for 10 rounds or until time is called. High score wins. Players switch roles at the end of each round.

Variations

• For beginning players, limit the total number of cards to less than 10.

• To make the standard game more challenging, change the rules so that a player/team must guess the cards with fewer samples in order to win points.

Block 'Em

This is a game for 2 players. Each player has 2 difference cards of the same rank and color.

Players take turns putting a card on the board. When all 4 cards are in position, players try to block their opponent from moving by sliding one of their cards, thus winning the game.

Look for a strategy to win.

Card Pick-Up Games

Materials

One deck of cards for each group.

Rules and Play

These logic games are for 2 players/teams. In each game, play starts form the left and proceeds in order to the right until all of the cards are removed. Play each game several times. Try to formulate a strategy to win.

Game 1. Place the cards Ace-Jack of a suit on the table. Each player is allowed to take 1 or 2 cards at a time. The player who takes the last card wins.

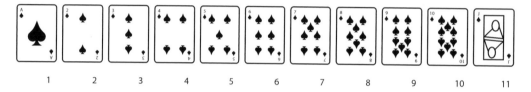

Game 2. Place the cards Ace-Queen of a suit on the table. Each player is allowed to take 1 or 2 cards at a time. The player who takes the last card wins.

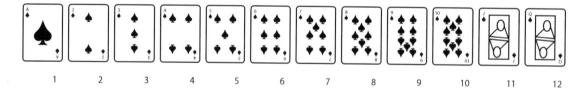

Game 3. Place the cards Ace-King of a suit on the table. Each player is allowed to take 1 or 2 cards at a time. The player who takes the last card wins.

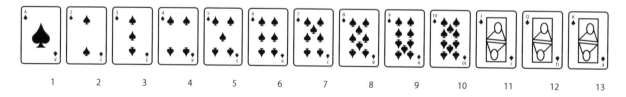

Materials

One deck of cards for each group (Aces = 1, Jacks = 11, Queens = 12, Kings = 13).
One *Give Me A Clue* record sheet for each player/team.

Rules and Play

1. This is a logic game for 2-4 players/teams.

2. The object of the game is to collect the most points by guessing hidden cards.

3. Play begins with the dealer drawing 2-4 cards, from a well-shuffled deck. After examining the cards, (s)he must give 2 clues that involve a math operation relating the cards. For example, if a Three of Diamonds, Five of Hearts and Jack of Clubs were drawn, the two clues might be.

   Clue #1 When you find the product of two of the cards, the answer is 15.
   Clue #2 When you double one of the cards, the answer is 22.

Next, players/teams take turns attempting to guess the value of the cards (note: it is not necessary to name the suit). The first player/team to name all 3 cards correctly wins a point. The player with the highest score after 10 round wins the game. Players/teams take turns dealing.

Variations

- For younger players, use 1 or 2 cards. Also, note face cards can be removed or given a value of 10 and operations restricted.

- To make the standard game more challenging, change the rules so that a player/team must also identify the suit for each card in order to win points.

- Change the scoring scheme to a formula. For example, the formula might be:
  Number of Points = (Number of Cards)(5 − Number of guesses)

Round	What were the cards?	How many guesses?	Points earned
1			
2			
3			
4			
5			
6			
7			
8			
9			
10			
		Final Score	

Round	What were the cards?	How many guesses?	Points earned
1			
2			
3			
4			
5			
6			
7			
8			
9			
10			
		Final Score	

I'll Give You Some Chances

Materials

One deck of cards for each group.
One *I'll Give You Some Chances* record sheet for each player/team.

Rules and Play

1. This is a logic game for 2-4 players/teams. Players/teams remove the Ten through King of each suit (Jokers = 0, Aces = 1).

2. The object of the game is to collect the most points by guessing a 2, 3 or 4 digit number.

3. Play begins with the dealer providing 2-4 cards, face down, to each player. A sample for a 3-card game is shown.

Chance	Guess	Clue
1	012	N
2	345	DD
3	543	DD
4	435	PP

Note: N(None), D(Digit), P(Place)

Next, the players take turns attempting to guess the 2-4-digit number represented by their cards. After each guess the dealer gives clues about the guess. Clues are given using this scheme.

N (None) Means none of the digits are correct.
D (Digit) Means one of the digits is correct, but it is in the wrong place.
P (Place) Means one of the digits is correct and in the right place.

4. Play continues until a player/team guesses the number. Points are awarded for each round based on the scheme shown on the record sheet.

5. Players change roles after each round.

6. The player/team with the highest score after 8 rounds wins.

Variations

• For younger players, use 2 cards and award 1 point for each correct guess.

• To make the standard game more challenging, change the rules so that a player/team must guess the number with fewer chances in order to win points.

I'll Give You Some Chances

Round	Secret Number	How many guesses?	Score Player 1	Score Player 2
1				
2				
3				
4				
5				
6				
7				
8				
9				
10				
		Final Scores		

2-Digit Game

Tries	Score
10	2
9	3
8	4
7	5
6	6
5	7
4	8
3	9
2	10
1	11

3-Digit Game

Tries	Score
15	2
14	3
13	4
12	5
11	6
10	7
9	8
etc.	etc.
1	16

4-Digit Game

Tries	Score
20	2
19	3
18	4
17	5
16	6
15	7
14	8
etc.	etc.
1	21

Materials

One deck of cards for each set of players/teams.
One *Street Hustler* score sheet.

Rules and Play

1. This is a logic game for 2 players/teams.

2. Players select 3 cards from the deck. Two of the cards should have the same rank. For example, 2 Jacks and a Nine might be selected.

3. The object of the game is to earn the most points.

4. The game begins by one player serving as the dealer. The dealer places the 3 cards face up on the table.

Next, the dealer turns the cards face down and quickly mixes them up for a maximum of 10 seconds. At the conclusion of the mixing, the dealer's opponent must attempt to guess the location of the Nine of Diamonds. If the player guesses which card is the Nine, (s)he gets one point.

5. Play continues for 10 rounds. The player/team with the most points after 10 rounds wins the game and becomes the dealer for the next game.

Variation

- Change the scoring rules so that players can specify the number of points on each round. For example, 1, 5, 10, 20, 50 or 100.

Name_____

Round	Score
1	
2	
3	
4	
5	
6	
7	
8	
9	
10	

Final Score	

Name_____

Round	Score
1	
2	
3	
4	
5	
6	
7	
8	
9	
10	

Final Score	

Name_____

Round	Score
1	
2	
3	
4	
5	
6	
7	
8	
9	
10	

Final Score	

Name_____

Round	Score
1	
2	
3	
4	
5	
6	
7	
8	
9	
10	

Final Score	

Name_____

Round	Score
1	
2	
3	
4	
5	
6	
7	
8	
9	
10	

Final Score	

Name_____

Round	Score
1	
2	
3	
4	
5	
6	
7	
8	
9	
10	

Final Score	

Materials

One deck of cards for each pair of players/teams.

Rules and Play

1. This is an inductive reasoning game for 2 players/teams.

2. Use 3 cards, two Aces and a Deuce. For example, the Ace of Clubs, the Two of Clubs and the Ace of Hearts.

3. The game begins by having the dealer shuffle the 3 cards and then place the cards face down, one in front of each player and one between them. At the signal of the dealer, players examine their own card. The first player to name the value of his/her opponent's card wins the round and earns 1 point. The first player to earn 10 points wins the game.

Variation

• Identify the color of the opponent's card.

Name_____

Round	Score
1	
2	
3	
4	
5	
6	
7	
8	
9	
10	

Final Score	

Name_____

Round	Score
1	
2	
3	
4	
5	
6	
7	
8	
9	
10	

Final Score	

Name_____

Round	Score
1	
2	
3	
4	
5	
6	
7	
8	
9	
10	

Final Score	

Yes, No, You Got It!

Materials

One deck of cards for each set of players (Jokers = 0, Aces = 1, Jacks = 11, Queens = 12, Kings = 13).

Rules and Play

1. This is a binary search strategy game for 2 or more players/teams.

2. Players/teams try to guess a card drawn at random by the dealer from a well-shuffled pack. Players take turns asking mathematical questions. The dealer responds to each question with one of these choices: Yes, No or You Got It!

3. For example, suppose the dealer chose a Four of Diamonds. A sample questioning sequence might go like this:

Is the card black?	No
Is the value of the card greater than 6?	No
Is the card greater than 3?	Yes
Is the card a five?	No
Is the card a six?	No
Is the card a heart?	No
Is the card the four of diamonds?	You Got It!

4. The player/team who uses the fewest number of guesses to determine a card wins the round. The winner of a round becomes the "dealer" for the next round. The first player/team to win 3 rounds wins the game.

Questions

1. What is the minimum number of possible guesses needed to win?

2. What is the minimum number of questions needed to guarantee that you know the value of the card?

3. If Jokers are not used, explain why the maximum number of guesses for any game is 52.

Variation

- Adjust the scoring scheme so that the player/team receives a score equal to the number value on the card that is guessed. The player/team with the highest total score at the end of the game wins.

Materials

One deck of cards for each set of players/teams.
Three small boxes for each set of players/teams.

Rules and Play

1. This is a place value and addition game for 2-5 players/teams. The object of the game is to make the largest number by tossing cards into place value boxes. Use the *Box Shot* record sheet to keep score.

2. First decide the number of rounds to play, the number of digits and the number of decimal places.

   Number of rounds? (2-12)
   Number of digits? (2-5)
   Number of decimal places? (0-3)

3. Use the cards Ace-Nine from the pack. Players/teams take turns drawing 3 cards from the pack and pitching the cards at the boxes from 3-4 feet away. The 3 boxes are labeled with the values .01, .1, and 1. Each player throws all 3 cards from the same side. After tossing the cards you must determine the score for that round by using the digit on the cards and the place value of the box. Your opponent(s) must check your answer. If your answer is incorrect, you forfeit your turn. If your answer is correct, you record your score and draw 3 cards on your next turn.

4. Scoring examples. If a player:
   draws a Five and throws it so that it lands in the .01 box (s)he receives .05 points.
   draws a Seven and throws it so that it lands in the 1 box (s)he receives 7 points.
   draws a Four and throws it so that it lands in the .1 box (s)he receives .4 points.
   draws a card and throws it so that it does not land in any of the three boxes, (s)he receives 0 points.

Variations

- Change the values of getting a card in the boxes. For example, 1, 10, and 100 or .1, 1, 10. Keep scoring rules the same.

- Increase the number of boxes so that games involving larger and smaller numbers can be played.

Name_____

Round	Score
1	
2	
3	
4	
5	
6	
7	
8	
9	
10	

Final Score	

Name_____

Round	Score
1	
2	
3	
4	
5	
6	
7	
8	
9	
10	

Final Score	

Name_____

Round	Score
1	
2	
3	
4	
5	
6	
7	
8	
9	
10	

Final Score	

Name_____

Round	Score
1	
2	
3	
4	
5	
6	
7	
8	
9	
10	

Final Score	

Name_____

Round	Score
1	
2	
3	
4	
5	
6	
7	
8	
9	
10	

Final Score	

Name_____

Round	Score
1	
2	
3	
4	
5	
6	
7	
8	
9	
10	

Final Score	

Math in the Cards
© IPMG Publishing

Materials

One deck of cards for each set of players/teams.

Rules and Play

1. This game is a reading whole numbers and decimals card game for 2 players/teams.

2. The dealer removes all of the face cards and Tens from the deck. Aces=1, Jokers=0.

3. The dealer places the cards face down in 2, 3, 4 or 5 piles, depending upon the maturity of the players and the difficulty level desired. There should be an equal number of cards in each pile.

4. Play begins by having the dealer turn over the top card in each pile. A sample is shown below. In this example, the first player to give the correct answer, 23, wins the cards. If a tie results, the top cards are placed at the bottom of each pile. If a player/team gives an incorrect answer, the opponent gets a "free" turn.

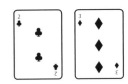

5. Play continues until the piles are depleted. The player/team with the most cards wins the game.

Variations

- Change the rules so that players/teams use a decimals template when playing the game. Two examples involving money and 3-digit decimals are shown.

- To make the game a cooperative endeavor, change the rules so that players take turns drawing and reading the numbers that are formed. If players can go through the entire pack without making an error, they win the game.

Fractions and Decimals In Between

Materials

One deck of cards for each player/team.
One *Fractions In Between or Decimals In Between* game board for each player/team.
Calculators are recommended for *Fractions In Between*.

Rules and Play

1. This is comparing whole numbers, fractions, decimals and integers game for 2 or more players/teams. Jokers=0, Aces=1, Jacks=11, Queens=12, Kings=13.

2. The object of the game is to get the most points. Players/teams earn points by building true statements using cards.

3. In *Fractions In Between*, use a complete deck and a *Fractions In Between* game board. Players take turns placing 6 cards, one at a time, on the board so that a true inequality is formed.

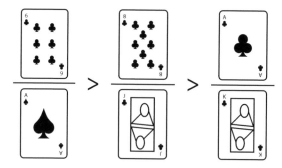

4. In *Decimals In Between*, the face cards and Tens are removed from the pack. Players take turns placing 3 cards, one at a time, on the *Decimals In Between* game board so that a true inequality is formed. An example is shown.

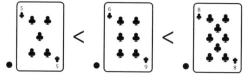

5. If the player/teams builds a true statement, (s)he get 1 point. If not, they get 0 points. The player or team with the high score at after one pass through the deck wins the game.

Variations

• For younger players, play without a game board using whole number values. Turn all cards face up and have players tell if the card in the middle has a value between the other two. If (s)he is correct, the player gets 3 cards. If the answer is correct, but the value in the middle is not between the others, the player gets 2 cards.

Fractions In Between

Use a full deck of cards, one at a time, on the game board. Then decide if the answer in the middle is between the other two values. You get 1 point if it is and 0 if it is not. The high score at the end of one pass through the deck is the winner.

Decimals In Between

Use the cards Ace through Nine. Deal 3 cards, one at a time, on the game board. Then decide if the decimal in the middle is between the other two values.

You get 1 point if it is and 0 if it is not. The high score after one pass through the deck wins.

Materials

One deck of cards for each set of players/teams.
One *Make A Buck* record sheet for each player/team.

Rules and Play

1. This is an addition of decimals game for 2 players/teams. In this game Aces = .01, Twos = .02, Threes = .03, ... Tens = .10, Jacks = .11, Queens = .12, Kings = .13.

2. The object of the game is to earn points by collecting cards whose total equals 1.00.

3. Play begins by dealing 10 cards to each player/team from well shuffled deck.

4. Players then take turns drawing and discarding one card at a time until the pack is depleted or one person has a total of 1.00.

5. The first player to accumulate 10 cards whose total is 1.00 (or $1.00) wins one point. If no player has 1.00 when the pack is exhausted, the player/team closest to 1.00 wins .5 of a point. The person with the highest score after 10 rounds wins the game.

Variations

- Change the value of the cards to whole numbers and play to 100 ($100). Change the name of the game to *Make A $100*.

- Change the value of the card to whole numbers and start at 100 ($100) and play to 0 using subtraction. Change the name of the game to *Countdown*.

- Change the value of the cards to integers. Use the black cards as positive numbers and the red cards are negative numbers. The object of the new game is to get close to 0. Change the name of the game to *Close Encounter*.

Name_____	
Round	Score
1	
2	
3	
4	
5	
6	
7	
8	
9	
10	

Final Score	

Name_____	
Round	Score
1	
2	
3	
4	
5	
6	
7	
8	
9	
10	

Final Score	

Name_____	
Round	Score
1	
2	
3	
4	
5	
6	
7	
8	
9	
10	

Final Score	

Name_____	
Round	Score
1	
2	
3	
4	
5	
6	
7	
8	
9	
10	

Final Score	

Name_____	
Round	Score
1	
2	
3	
4	
5	
6	
7	
8	
9	
10	

Final Score	

Name_____	
Round	Score
1	
2	
3	
4	
5	
6	
7	
8	
9	
10	

Final Score	

Materials

One deck of cards for each set of players/teams.
One record sheet for each player/team.

Rules and Play

1. This is a percent mental math card game for teams.

2. The game is played using a full deck (Jokers = 0, Aces = 1, Jacks = 11, Queens = 12, Kings = 13).

3. The object of the game is to be the first team to solve all the problems correctly and decode the secret occupation.

4. The problems on the following page are used for the game. In this game players must work as a relay team. In this relay, each player on a team does one percent problem and passes the sheet on to the next person. The last person fills in the blanks at the bottom of the page to reveal the secret occupation. Points are awarded according to the following scheme.

   Correct Solution(s): 1 point per problem
   Correct Occupation: 1 point per letter
   Fastest Completion Time: 1 point

5. High score wins.

Variations

• Create a new set of problems and answers for a secret occupation.

Code Letters	Problems	Answers
R	What is 5% of the Ten of Hearts?	_____
N	What is 50% of the Ten of Hearts?	_____
B	What is 25% of the Ten of Hearts?	_____
O	What is 75% of the Ten of Hearts?	_____
U	What is 10% of the Ten of Hearts?	_____
T	What is 1% of the Ten of Hearts?	_____
M	6% of the Queen of Spades numberical value is	_____
G	11% of the Queen of Spades numberical value is	_____
A	15% of the Queen of Spades numberical value is	_____
E	1/2% of the Queen of Spades numberical value is	_____
I	2% of the Queen of Spades numberical value is	_____
S	20% of the Queen of Spades numberical value is	_____

———   ———   ———   ———   ———   ———   ———   ———   ———   ———
1.8   1.32   .5   7.5   5   7.5   .72   .24   2.4   .1

Materials

One deck of cards for each set of players/teams.

Rules and Play

1. This is a comparing and addition of fractions game for two or more players. Players try to get as close to 2 or 22 as possible. In this game Jokers = 0, Aces = 1 or 11, Jacks = 1/2, Queens = 1/2, Kings = 1/2.

2. This game is played much like 21 except that players can start or stop whenever they wish.

3. Players may be over or under 2 or 22. The player closest to 2 or 22 wins the round and earns 1 point. In the event of a tie, both players receive 1 point. The first player to earn 10 points wins the game.

Variations

- Change the value of the cards so that each black card is a positive integer and each red card is a negative integer.

- Change the value of the cards so that Tens = 1/10, Jacks = 1/11, Queens = 1/12, Kings = 1/13. Allow calculator use.

- Change the rules so that players keep all the cards when they win. The player/team with the most cards after one pass through the deck wins.

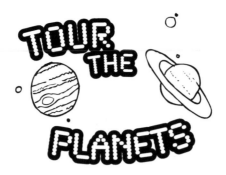

Materials

One deck of cards for each group. Aces = 1, Jacks = 11, Queens = 12 and Kings = 13.
One *Tour the Planets* game board.
One record sheet for each group.
One marker for each player.

Rules and Play

1. This is an interdisciplinary card game for 2-4 players. Players select the operation. The object is to be the first player to travel from the sun to all 9 planets by solving problems and answering questions.

2. The dealer shuffles the cards and puts them face down on the playing area.

3. Players take turns drawing 2 cards and stating the answer to the problem by using +, -, x, or /. If the answer is incorrect, the turn is over. If the answer is correct, that player's marker is moved to that planet's position from the sun and allowed to stay if (s)he can identify the name of the planet. If either answer is incorrect, the marker is returned to the Sun position on the game board. For example, a player drew a Six and Three. (S)he could find the sum or difference and then move to the third or ninth planet. If (s)he moved to the ninth planet and identified it correctly as Pluto, his or her score for that round would be 10, 9 points for the math problem and 1 point for the correct name of the planet. Players are allowed to be on the same planet without being sent back to the Sun. Players may return to a planet more than once. Used cards are placed in a discard pile.

4. If the pack is depleted before the game ends, the dealer shuffles the discards, places them face down in a new pack and play continues.

5. Play continues until one person/team visits all 9 planets or time is called. If a person/team visits all 9 planets, (s)he/they win. If time expires, the person/team with the highest score wins.

Variations

• Change the scoring rules. One point for the correct math, one point for the correct planet name. High score wins.

• Change the rules so players must race from the sun to Pluto. The player/team to arrive first wins. This can be played drawing 1 or 2 cards.

• Change the rules so a player must start at the sun and travel to Pluto in order, or vice versa.

• Change the rules so a player must start at the sun and travel to Pluto in order or vice versa, but if 2 markers land on the same planet, the last arrival stays and the other person is sent back to start.

Pack

Discard

Round	Cards Drawn	Math Answer	Planet Name	Score
			Final Score	

Materials

One deck of cards for each group. Aces = 1, Jacks = 11, Queens = 12 and Kings = 13.
One *Tour the USA* game board.
One record sheet for each group.
One marker for each player.

Rules and Play

1. This is an interdisciplinary card game for 2-3 players. Players select the operation. The object is to be the first player to go to all 50 states by answering questions.

2. The dealer shuffles the cards and puts them face down on the playing area.

3. Players take turns drawing 2 cards and stating the answer to the problem by using +, -, x or /. If the answer is incorrect, the turn is over. If the answer is correct, that player's marker is advanced to the next state, in alphabetical order, and allowed to stay if (s)he can name the state and the state capitol. If either answer is incorrect, the marker is returned to the pervious position on the board. Players are allowed to be in the same state without being sent back to start. Players may return to a state more than once. Used cards are placed in a discard pile.

4. If the pack is depleted before the game ends, the dealer shuffles the discards, places them face down in a new pack, and play continues.

5. Play continues until one player/team visits all 50 states or time is called. If a player/team visits all 50 states, (s)he/they win. If time expires, the player with the highest score wins.

Variations

- Change the rules so a player must solve the math problem, name the next state and name the state's capitol.

- Change the scoring rules. One point for the correct math, one point for the correct state and one point for the correct capitol.

Pack

Discard

Round	Cards Drawn	Math Answer	State Name	Abb.	Capitol	Score

MathGeekMama.com

Card Patterns

Complete Each Pattern

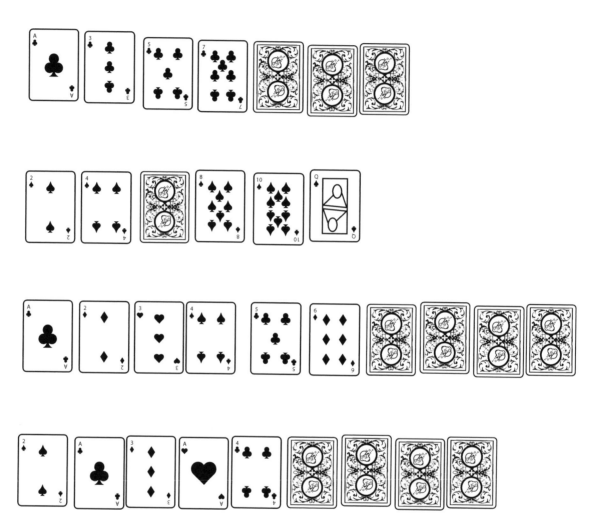

Make up your own card pattern and test it on a partner. Record the pattern and answer below.

Consecutive Numbers

1. Place the value of Ace through Five of a suit so that no two consecutive numbers are connected by a segment in the pentagon diagram. Ace = 1. Record your answer.

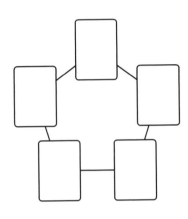

3. Place the value of Ace through Seven of a suit so that no two consecutive numbers are connected by a segment in the heptagon diagram. Ace = 1. Record your answer.

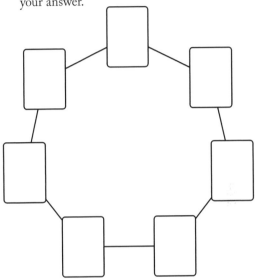

2. Place the value of Ace through Six of a suit so that no two consecutive numbers are connected by a segment in the hexagon diagram. Ace = 1. Record your answer.

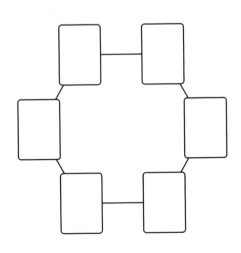

4. Place the value of Ace through Eight of a suit so that no two consecutive numbers are connected by a segment in the octagon diagram. Ace = 1. Record your answer.

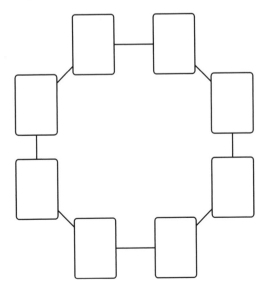

Math in the Cards
© IPMG Publishing

MathGeekMama.com

Consecutive Numbers

5. Place the value of the Ace through Seven of a suit so that no two consecutive numbers are connected by a segment. Aces = 1. Record your answer.

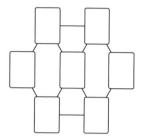

6. Place the value of the cards Ace through Eight of a suit so that no two consecutive numbers are connected by a segment. Ace = 1. Record your answer.

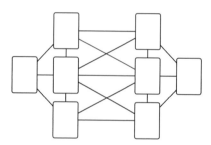

7. Place the value of the Ace through Ten of a suit so that no two consecutive numbers are connected by a segment. Ace= 1. Record your answer.

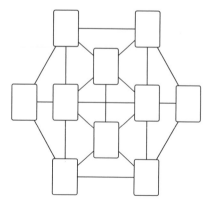

8. Place the value of the cards Ace through Jack of a suit so that no two consecutive numbers are connected by a segment. Ace= 1, Jack= 11. Record your answer.

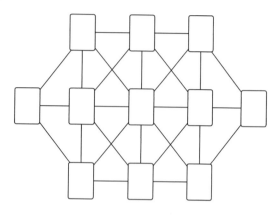

9. Nicky made up a consecutive numbers problem using the cards Ace through Ten of a suit. The challenge is to place the value of the cards so that no two consecutive numbers are connected. Solve Nicky's puzzle.

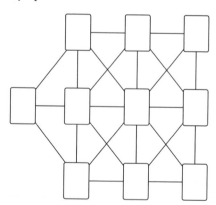

10. Make up your own consecutive numbers card puzzle. Record your problem and answer.

Finding Sums

1. Place the value of the cards Ace through Five of a suit on the pentagon diagram so that no two cards connected by a segment have the same sum. Ace= 1. Record your answer.

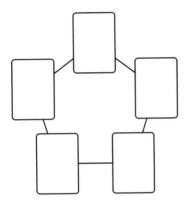

3. Arrange the values of the cards Ace through Queen of a suit on the hexagon diagram so that the sum of the cards on every side of the hexagon is different. Ace= 1, Jack= 11, Queen= 12. Record your answer.

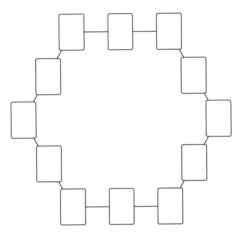

2. Place the value of the cards Ace through Six of a suit on the hexagon diagram so that no two cards connected by a segment have he same sum. Ace= 1. Record your answer.

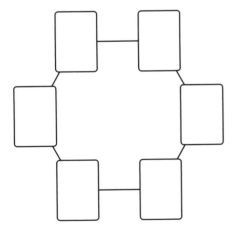

4. Use the cards Ace through Seven of a suit. Place the value of the cards so that the sum of the values of the cards in each connected row, column and diagonal is 12. Ace= 1. Record your answer.

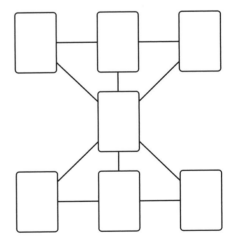

Finding Sums

5. Use the odd cards of a suit. Place the value of the cards so that the sum of the values of the cards in each line is 21. Ace= 1, Jack= 11, King= 13. Record your answer.

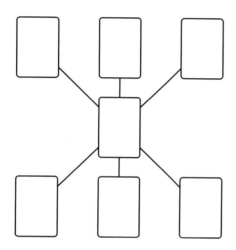

6. Use the cards Ace through Five of a suit. Place the value of the cards so that the sum of the values of the cards in any straight line is the same. Ace= 1. Record your answer.

7. Use the cards Ace through Jack of a suit. Place the value of the cards so that the sum of the values of the cards in any straight line is 18. Ace= 1, Jack= 11. Record your answer.

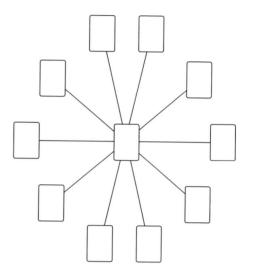

8. Make up your own connecting cards and finding sums card puzzle. Record your problem and answer.

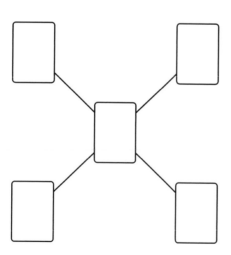

More Finding Sums

Materials

One deck of cards.
More Finding Sums Card Puzzles template.

Challenge

1. Use the cards Ace through Seven of any suit. Arrange the cards on the *More Finding Sums Card Puzzles* template so that the sum of the cards in a line is 10. Record your answer and describe how you solve the problem.

2. Make up your own card puzzle involving products, differences or quotients.

Variations

Use these cards to find more sums:

Ace through Seven to find 12.
Ace through Seven to find 14.
Joker (0) through Six to find 7, 9 and 11.
Two through Eight to find 13, 15 and 17.
Three through Nine to find 16, 18 and 20.
Four through Ten to find 19, 21 and 23.
Five through Jack (11) to find 22, 24 and 26.
Six through Queen (12) to find 25, 27 and 29.
Seven through King (13) to find 28, 30 and 32.

More Finding Sums

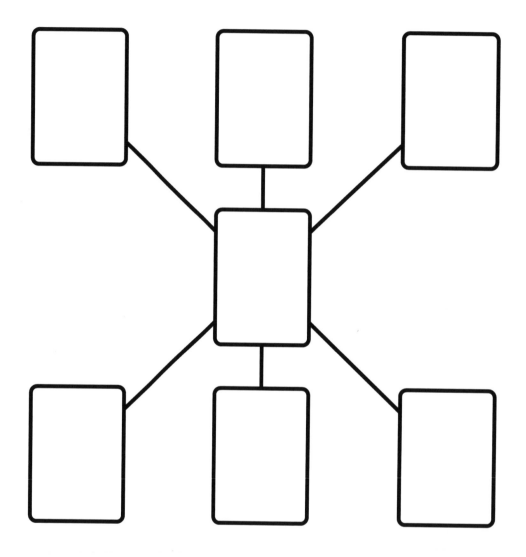

Math in the Cards
© IPMG Publishing

Five-Pointed Star

Instructions

1. Use the Ace through Ten of a suit. Place the value of the cards on the star so that no line of 4 cards has the same sum. Record your answer.

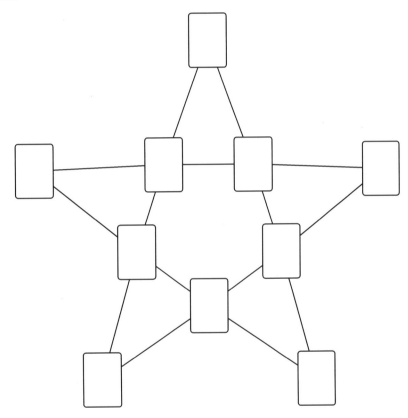

2. Use three Deuces, 2 Fours, 2 Sixes and 3 Eights. Place the value of the cards on the star so that the sum of each line of 4 cards is 20. Record your answer.

3. Use the Ace through Ten of a suit. Place the value of the cards on the star so that the sum of each line of 4 cards is the same. Is it possible? Explain.

4. Make up your own *Five-Pointed Star* card puzzle. Record your problem and answer.

Six-Pointed Star

Instructions

1. Use the Ace through Queen of a suit. Place the value of the cards on the star so that the sum of any line of 4 cards is 26. Ace = 1, Jack = 11, Queen = 12. Record your answer.

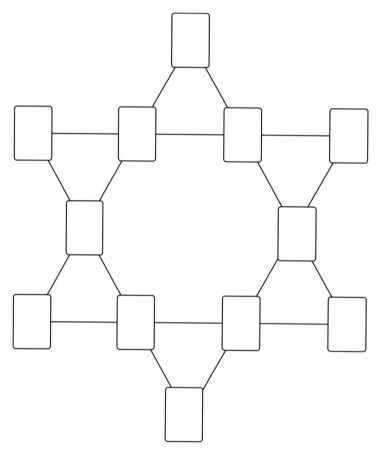

2. Use the 2 through King of a suit. Jack= 11, Queen= 12, King= 13. Place the value of the cards on the star so that the sum of any line of 4 cards is the same. Record the sum of each line of 4 cards and the placement of the cards on the diagram.

3. Use 4 Fours, 4 Sixes and 4 Eights. Place the value of the cards on the star so that the sum of any line of 4 cards is 24. Record your answer.

4. Make up your own *Six-Pointed Star* card puzzle. Record your problem and answer.

Bullseye

Instructions

Find the operation and hidden cards used to make each puzzle.

1.

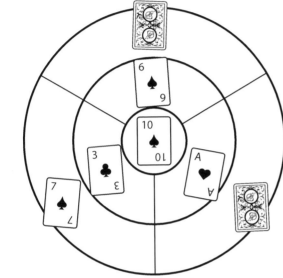

2.

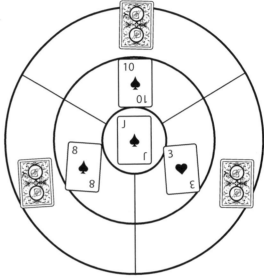

3.

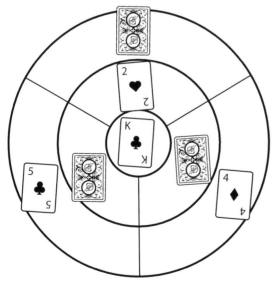

4.

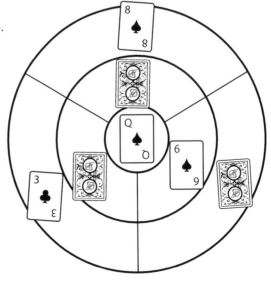

Bullseye

Instructions

Find the operation and hidden cards used to make each puzzle.

5.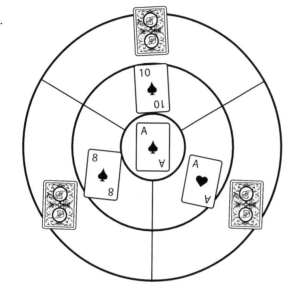

6.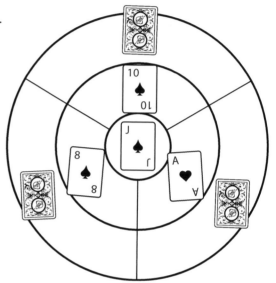

7.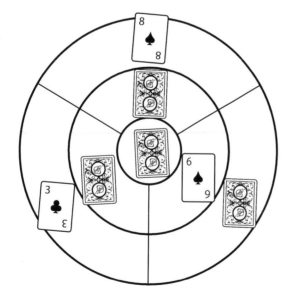

8.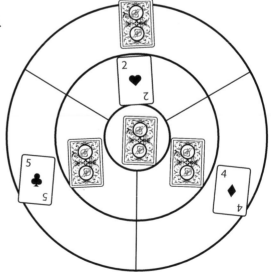

Operation Table Card Puzzles

Instructions

Fill in each missing card and answer.

Puzzle 1

+	A♠	
	10	15
7♣		

Puzzle 2

X		3♠
8♦		
9♣	54	

Puzzle 3

−	9♣	5♠
	4	
	2	

Puzzle 4

X		3♦
	100	
7♣		

Puzzle 5

−	7♠	
J♥		3
		3

Puzzle 6

+		
		18
Q♦	20	21

Puzzle 7

−	2♠	
	7	
Q♥		4

Puzzle 8

+	8♣	A♥
5♦		
		14

Puzzle 9

X		7♦
9♣	72	
4♣		

Guess My Rule Card Puzzles

Instructions

We can make up our own card table operations. For example, we could multiply the number on the left side of the table by the top number and then add 1. We can even make up our own operation symbol L x T + 1. For each problem, figure out how the operation works. Then, fill in the missing cards and answers.

Puzzle 1

LxT+1	A♣	3♣
5♠		16
7♦		

Puzzle 2

L+T+3	7♠	3♥
8♠		
9♣		

Puzzle 3

2xL-T	A♠	J♥
		1
		11

Puzzle 4

LxT-1		3♣
	99	
7♠		

Puzzle 5

L+T-5	7♠	
J♣		13
		3

Puzzle 6

LxT+1		
	6	8
Q♦	9	

Puzzle 7

L/T+5	2♥	
	9	
Q♠		8

Puzzle 8

2(L+T)	8♠	A♥
5♣		
		28

Puzzle 9

		7♠
9♦		
4♣		

Border Patrol Card Puzzles

Instructions

1. Try to beat each challenge time. Fill in each cell with the value of a card from Joker through King (Joker = 0, Ace = 1, Jack = 11, Queen = 12, King = 13).

2. The cards in each row should add to the answers on the left and right. The cards in each column should add to the answers on the top and bottom. The cards in each major diagonal should also be totaled.

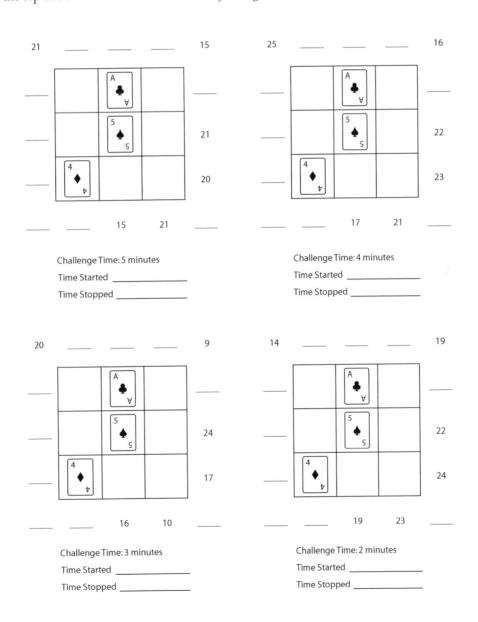

Challenge Time: 5 minutes

Time Started _____

Time Stopped _____

Challenge Time: 4 minutes

Time Started _____

Time Stopped _____

Challenge Time: 3 minutes

Time Started _____

Time Stopped _____

Challenge Time: 2 minutes

Time Started _____

Time Stopped _____

More Border Patrol Card Puzzles

Instructions

1. Try to beat each challenge time. Fill in each cell with the value of a card from Joker through King (Joker = 0, Ace = 1, Jack = 11, Queen = 12, King = 13).

2. Fill in each empty cell with the value of a card from Ace through Nine. Aces=1.

3. The cards in each row should total to the answers on the right. The cards in each column should total the answers on the bottom. Cards in each major diagonal should total to the answers in the upper and lower right.

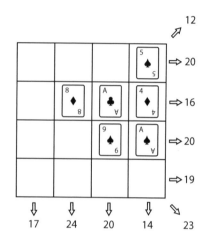

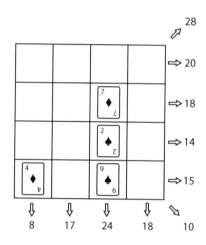

Challenge Time: 10 minutes

Time Started _____

Time Stopped _____

Challenge Time: 10 minutes

Time Started _____

Time Stopped _____

4. Make up your own *Border Patrol Puzzle*. Record your problem and answer below.

Cards, Triangles and Patterns

Instructions

For each problem, study the figures and look for a pattern. Then identify the mystery card and record the function. The first problem has been completed for you. Write your rule algebraically using T=top card, L=lower left card and R=lower right card.

1.

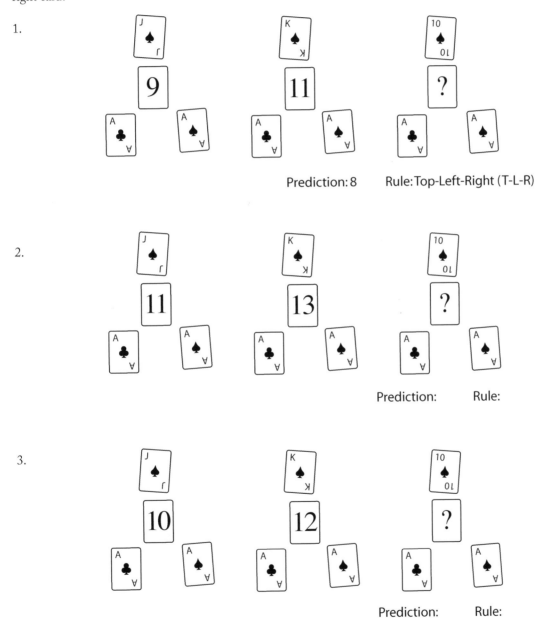

Prediction: 8   Rule: Top-Left-Right (T-L-R)

2.

Prediction: Rule:

3.

Prediction: Rule:

Cards, Triangles and Patterns

4.

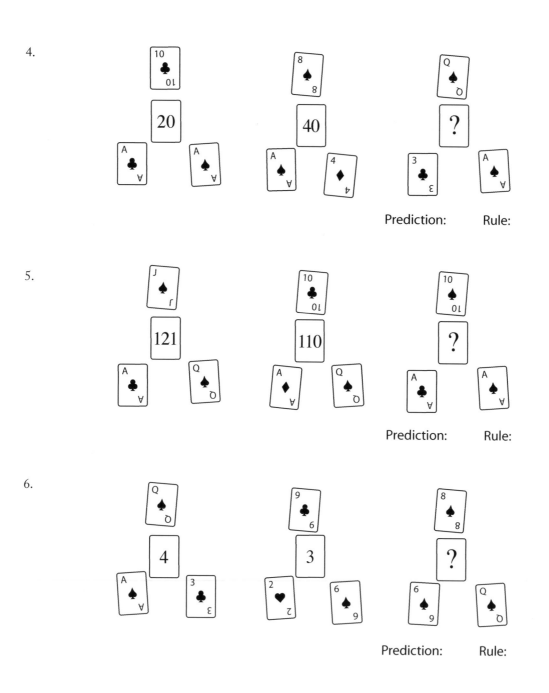

Prediction: Rule:

5.

Prediction: Rule:

6.

Prediction: Rule:

Nine-Card Logic Puzzles

Instructions

Use the cards Ace through Seven of all suits. Place 3 cards across so that their products match the numbers in right margin of the page.

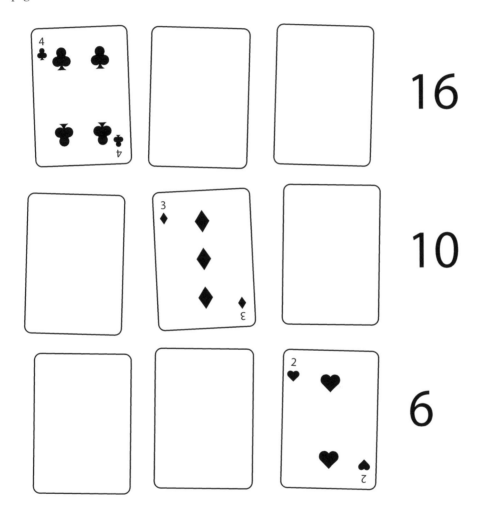

16

10

6

Nine-Card Logic Puzzles

Instructions

Use the cards Ace through Seven of all suits. Place 3 cards across so that their products match the numbers in right margin of the page.

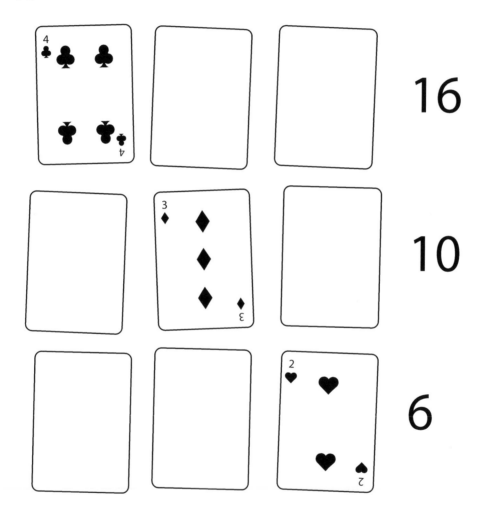

16

10

6

TIDY SUM

CARD PUZZLE

Use the cards Ace through Nine of a suit. Place the cards so that the correct sum is formed. Find all the possible answers.

+

_____

10

TIDY SUM
CARD PUZZLE II

Use the cards Ace through Nine of a suit. Place the cards so that the correct sum is formed. Find all the possible answers.

+

100

TIDY SUM
CARD PUZZLE III

Use the cards Ace through Nine of a suit. Place the cards so that the correct sum is formed. Find all the possible answers.

1000

Logic Puzzles

Materials

One deck of ordinary cards.

Rules

Place 3 Fives, 3 Threes and 3 Aces on the Logic Puzzle template.

Challenges

1. Select 3 cards to get a total of 15.

2. Select 5 cards to get a total of 15.

3. Select 6 cards to get a total of 16.

4. Select 4 cards to get a total of 10.

5. Select 3 cards to get a total of 10.

6. Change the position of the Nine cards so that the sum of each row, column and diagonal is the same.

7. Make up your own card logic puzzle. Use the Logic Puzzle template on the following pages.

Variations

- Use a 3x3 board, sets of 3 cards and a new total.

- Use a 3x4 board, sets of 3 Aces, 3 Threes, 3 Fives and 3 Nines and a total of 21. Use the template on the following pages.

- Use a 3x4 board, sets of 3 cards and a new total. Use the templates on the following pages.

LOGIC
PUZZLES

Windmill Card Puzzles

1. Place four of a kind so that 2 cards connected by a segment have the same sum. Record your answer and any patterns you notice.

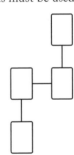

2. Suppose the sum of 2 cards connected by any segment is 3. What cards must be used?

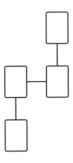

3. Suppose the sum of 2 cards connected by any segment is 13. What cards must be used?

4. Suppose the sum of 2 cards connected by any segment is 6. What cards must be used?

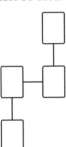

1

5. Suppose the sum of 2 cards connected by any segment is the same. What cards must be used?

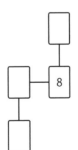

8

Windmill Card Puzzles

6. Suppose the product of 2 cards connected by any segment is 130. What cards must be used?

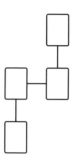

7. Suppose the sum of 2 cards connected by any segment is 13. What cards must be used?

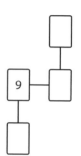

8. Use the cards Ace through Eight of a suit. Place the cards so that the sum of the values of any 3 cards in each row, or column is 15.

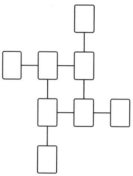

9. Use the cards Two through King of a suit. Place the cards so that the sum of the values of the cards in each line is 30 (Jacks=11, Queen=12, King=13).

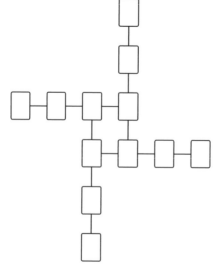

Take A Walk

Suppose 9 cards are dealt as shown

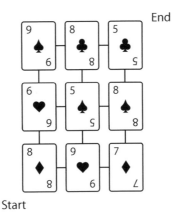

For each problem, begin at start, stop at end. Retracing is not allowed.

1. Follow the paths to collect 5 cards.

     a. What is the highest total possible?
     b. What is the lowest total possible?
     c. Is there an answer that is unique?

2. Follow the paths to collect 7 cards.

     a. What is the highest total possible?
     b. What is the lowest total possible?
     c. Is there an answer that is unique?

3. Suppose we change the operation to multiplication. What are the new answers for problems 1 and 2?

4. Suppose the black cards are positive integers and the red cards are negative integers. What are the new answers for problems 1 and 2?

5. How many different ways are there to walk from "start" to "end"?

Variations

- Use the cards Five through Nine of any suit. Deal 9 cards in a square array as shown.

- Use the cards Ace through Nine or Ace through King of any suit.

- Use larger arrays, 4 x 4, 4 x 5 and 5 x 5.

Spider Math Paths

Suppose 13 cards are dealt as shown.

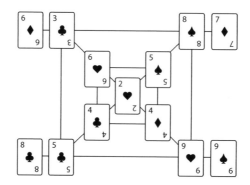

For each problem, retracing a web path is allowed, but the value of the card(s) can counted only once.

1. Suppose you start at any position on the web and collect any 5 cards.

    a. What is the highest total possible?
    b. What is the lowest total possible?
    c. Is there an answer that is unique?

2. Suppose you must start at any corner card and follow the web to collect 4 cards.

    a. What is the highest total possible?
    b. What is the lowest total possible?
    c. Is there an answer that is unique?

3. Suppose we change the operation to multiplication. What are the new answers for problems 1 and 2?

4. Suppose the black cards are positive integers and the red cards are negative integers. What are the new answers for problems 1 and 2?

Variations

- Start with a score of 52 and use subtraction.

- Start with a score of 52 and use division. Calculators allowed.

- Do not allow retracing of paths.

- Collect less than 5 cards or more than 5 cards.

- Place 13 new cards on the Spider Math Board and find the answers to problems 1-4.

Fancy Footwork Featuring Fours Card Puzzles

$$(4 + 4 + 4) / 4 = 3 \qquad 4 / 4 + 4 + 4 = 9$$

The sentence above shows how three and nine can be formed using exactly four 4s, addition and division. The numbers from 1-50 can be formed using four 4s. You may use addition, subtraction, multiplication, division, exponents, decimal points, square roots, factorials or any other legal math maneuver to solve these puzzles. See how many you can find. Record your results below.

1. _____
2. _____
3. $(4 + 4 + 4) / 4$
4. _____
5. _____
6. _____
7. _____
8. _____
9. $4 / 4 + 4 + 4$
10. _____
11. _____
12. _____
13. _____
14. _____
15. _____
16. _____
17. _____
18. _____
19. _____
20. _____
21. _____
22. _____
23. _____
24. _____
25. _____

26. _____
27. _____
28. _____
29. _____
30. _____
31. _____
32. _____
33. _____
34. _____
35. _____
36. _____
37. _____
38. _____
39. _____
40. _____
41. _____
42. _____
43. _____
44. _____
45. _____
46. _____
47. _____
48. _____
49. _____
50. _____

Shifting Cards Puzzles

1. Place 12 cards face down like the example below.

Move 2 cards so that each row and column has an even number of cards.

2. Place 10 cards face down like the example below.

Move 2 cards so that each row and column has an even number of cards.

3. Make up your own shifting cards puzzle. Record your problem and answer.

Switching Cards Puzzles

Rules and Play

1. For each problem, place the cards face up in a line as shown below. Next, arrange the cards so that all the numbers are in order from smallest on the left to largest on the right by switching adjacent cards. Then answer the question that follows (Ace = 1, Jack = 11, Queen = 12, King = 13).

a. How many moves did it take to complete the task?

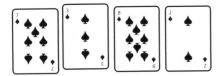

b. How many moves did it take to complete the task?

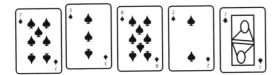

c. How many moves did it take to complete the task?

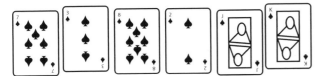

d. How many moves did it take to complete the task?

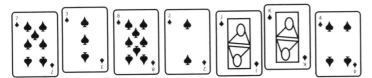

e. How many moves did it take to complete the task?

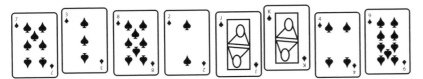

Switching Cards Puzzles

f. How many moves did it take to complete the task?

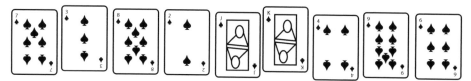

g. How many moves did it take to complete the task?

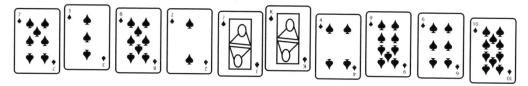

h. How many moves did it take to complete the task?

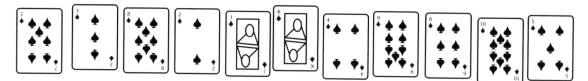

i. How many moves did it take to complete the task?

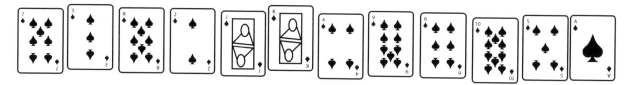

j. How many moves did it take to complete the task?

2. Record the information you accumulated in Exercise 1 below. What patterns do you notice?

Number of Cards	4	5	6	7	8	9	10	11	12	13
Number of Cards										

Magic Square Card Puzzles

Materials

One deck of ordinary playing cards

Rules and Play

Use a Joker and the cards Ace through Eight of any suit. Create a 3 x 3 array with the cards, similar to the example below. Arrange the cards so that the sum of each row, column and diagonal is 12. Note the value of the Joker is 0.

Variations

- Use these cards:
  Ace through Nine of any suit
  Two through Ten of any suit
  Three through Jack of any suit
  Four through Queen of any suit
  Five through King of any suit

  Find these sums:
  15
  18
  21
  24
  27

- Make up your own card puzzle!

Circles and Reasoning
Card Puzzle

Materials

One deck of cards

Challenge

Arrange 4 cards on the mat so that the sum of the cards on each circle is the same. What patterns do you notice?

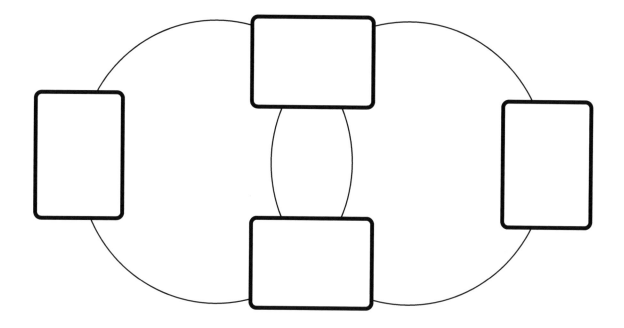

Circles and Reasoning
Card Puzzle II

Challenge

Use one deck of cards (Jokers = 0, Aces = 1, Jacks = 11, Queens = 12, Kings = 13). Place the value of 6 cards on the template so the sum of the cards on each circle is the same. Record your answer.

Variation

• Place 6 cards on the template so the product of the cards on each circle is the same.

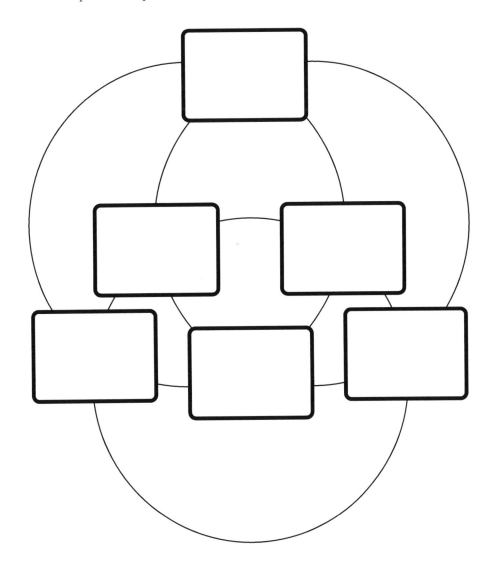

Circles and Reasoning
Card Puzzle III

Challenge

Use one deck of cards (Jokers = 0, Aces = 1, Jacks = 11, Queens = 12, Kings = 13). Place the value of 4 cards on the template so the sum of the cards on each circle is the same. Record your answer.

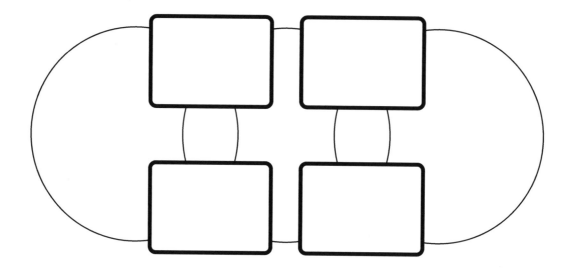

Circles and Reasoning
Card Puzzle IV

Challenge

Use one deck of cards (Jokers = 0, Aces = 1, Jacks = 11, Queens = 12, Kings = 13). Place the value of 6 cards on the template so the sum of the cards on each circle is the same. Record your answer.

Variation

• Place 6 cards on the template so the product of the cards on each circle is the same.

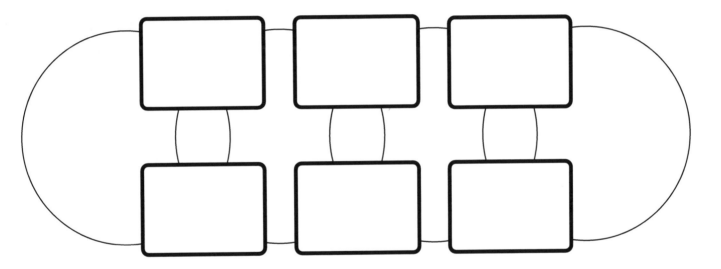

Olympic Rings Card Puzzle

Challenge

Use one deck of cards (Jokers = 0, Aces = 1, Jacks = 11, Queens = 12, Kings = 13). Place the value of 12 cards on the template so the sum of the cards on each circle is the same. Record your answer.

Variation

• Place 12 cards on the template so the product of the cards on each circle is the same.

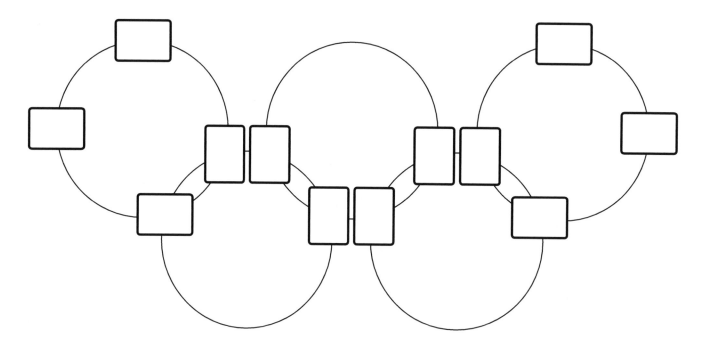

Secret Messages

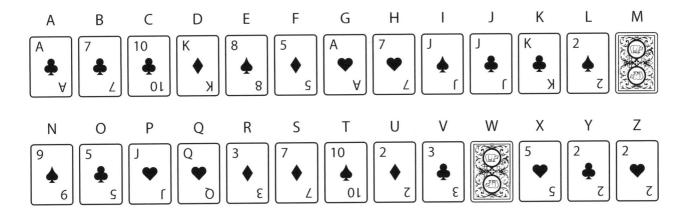

1. Use the card code (above) to figure out the message below. Record your answer..

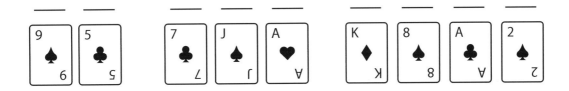

2. Use the card code to create a puzzle with each message:

     a. Call me
     b. It's a draw
     c. Shuffle along
     d. Wear a suit
     e. It's a good deal
     f. You're bluffing

3. Use the card code to create your own secret message.

Check Out The Symbols

Problems

1. Estimate the number of club, diamond, heart and spade symbols that are printed on the face up side of a 52-card deck of playing cards. Then check your estimate using a deck of cards.

   Estimate =

   Actual =

2. How many cards have more symbols than the face cards?

3. What fraction of the cards have fewer than 4 symbols?

4. What percent of the cards have exactly 4 symbols?

Place Value

1. Use the cards Ace through Nine of a suit. Imagine someone has a secret 3-digit number. Use these clues to find the number and the cards.

   The hundreds digit is half the ones digit.
   The sum of the tens digit and the ones digit is nine.

2. Use the cards Ace through Nine of a suit. Imagine someone has a secret 4-digit number. Use these clues to find the number and the cards.

   The ones digit is six times the tens digit.
   The hundreds digit is twice the tens digit.
   The thousands digit is three times the hundreds digit.
   The sum of all four digits is 15.

3. Use the cards Ace through Nine of a suit. Imagine someone has a secret 5-digit number. Use these clues to find the number and the cards.

   The ten thousands digit is three times the hundreds digit.
   The sum of the hundreds digit and the thousands digit is the ones digit.
   The thousands digit is two times the hundreds digit.
   The sum of all four digits is 31.

4. Make up your own place value card puzzle. Record your problem and answer.

Dissecting A Card

Materials

One pair of scissors for each player/team.
One piece of metric graph paper for each player/team.
One copy of the card dissection puzzle for each player/team.

Exercises

Dissection puzzles have been popular for hundreds of years. In this activity we explore how a card can be dissected and then analyzed using math.

1. Cut out the large *Dissecting A Card* Puzzle on page 186. Then use the card pieces to make the Ace of Clubs on page 187. Record your results.

2. Identify the polygon name of each card piece.

A _____

B _____

C _____

D _____

E _____

F _____

G _____

H _____

I _____

J _____

K _____

L _____

M _____

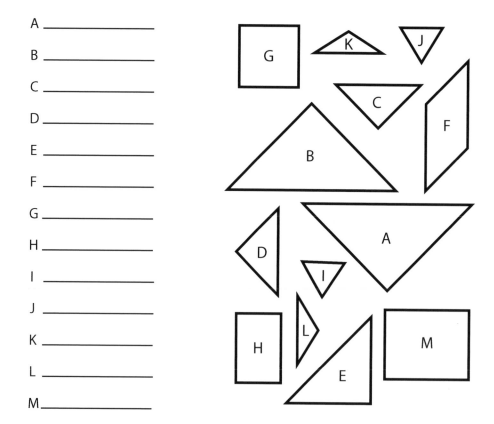

Dissecting A Card

Exercises

3. Use the 2 large triangles to make a square. What is the perimeter and area of the square?

4. Use triangles D and E to make a square. What is the perimeter and area of the square?

5. Use the pieces A, B, C, D, E, F and G to form a square on a square centimeter grid. Sketch your answer. Then find the perimeter and area of the square.

6. What is the area of each card piece in the square centimeters?

7. Suppose the rectangle that you formed to make the card is one whole or 100%. What fraction and percent of the whole card is each piece? Record your answers in the table below.

A _____

B _____

C _____

D _____

E _____

F _____

G _____

H _____

I _____

J _____

K _____

L _____

M _____

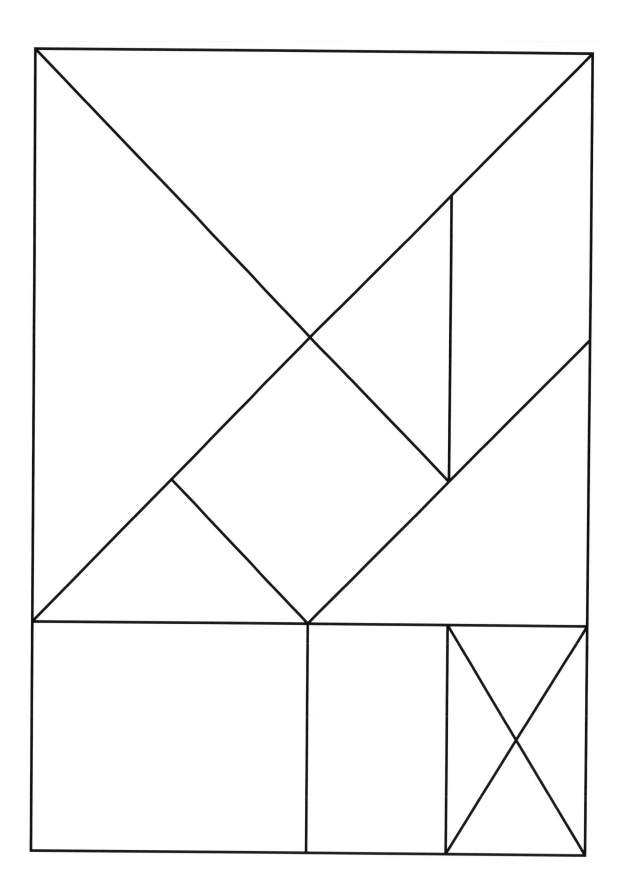

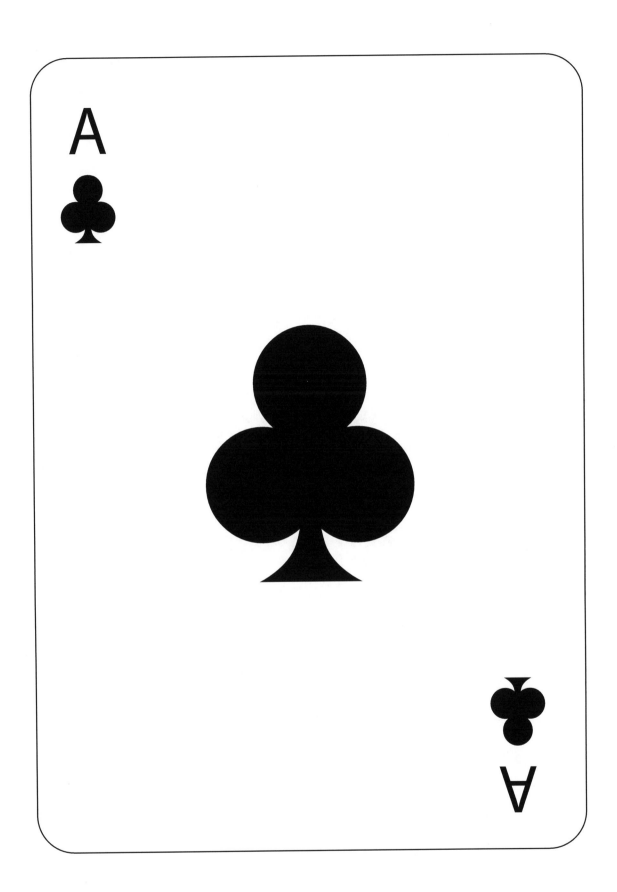

An Amazing 3-Stack Card Trick

Try this trick and then answer the questions that follow.

In this trick, Ace = 1, Jack = 11, Queen = 12, and King = 13.

1. Shuffle the cards.

2. Turn over the top card. Suppose it is a Four. Place the Four in a pile and proceed to count up to the King (13). Be sure to place the cards on top of one another in the pile. Note the cards will not usually be in order as you count, but proceed as though they are until you reach 13.

3. After you have reached 13, start a new pile. For example, suppose you drew a Jack. You would start the second pile with a Jack (11) and place down two cards to reach the King (13) again.

4. Repeat this process until you cannot count up to 13 to complete a pile. Put these cards aside. You will now have several piles. Select any 3 of the piles and turn them over.

5. Next, remove the remaining piles of cards and combine them with the cards you put aside.

6. Now turn over the top cards on 2 of the 3 piles. Find the sum and then add 10. For example, supposed the cards were a Nine and a Four. Add 9 + 4 and we get 13. Add 10 more and we get 23.

7. Finally, take your answer and count that number of cards into the discard pack. In our example this would be 23. The number of remaining cards in the discard pack is the value of the card to be turned over in the third pile. Turn over the top card and the card value will match the number of remaining cards in the discard pile. In our example, there are 5 cards remaining, so the value of the top card in the third pile will be 5.

Questions

1. Suppose the top card in a stack is a Five.

   a. How many cards will be in the stack?

   b. What is the general rule for the number of cards in the stack if you know the top card?

An Amazing 3-Stack
Card Trick

2. Why does this trick work? Use diagrams in your explanation.

3. Sharon wondered if the trick would work with less than 3 piles or more than 3 piles. For example, she used the usual rules, but selected 2 piles rather than 3 and turned over the top card on just one pile. Then she tried the trick with 4 piles. She turned over the top card on 3 piles and was able to predict the value of the card on top of the fourth pile. She found that a different adjustment amount was needed for each trick. Try her idea. What are the adjustment amounts? Can her idea be extended to 5, 6, 7, 8, 9 or 10 piles? Explain.

4. Mike experimented with the 3-stack card trick. He used the usual rules but decided to change the number of cards in the deck. For example, instead of Ace – King, he used Ace – Queen, Ace – Jack, Ace – Ten, Ace – Nine, etc. He said the trick still works, but that he needed to change the adjustment amount. His adjustment amount formula is shown below.

   Adjustment amount = (Total number of cards used/4) – 3.

   a. Use the formula to complete the table below. Then try several examples to test his conjecture. Is he correct?

Cards Used	Adjustment Amount
Ace - King	10
Ace - Queen	
Ace - Jack	
Ace - Ten	
Ace - Nine	
Ace - Eight	
Ace - Seven	
Ace- Six	
Ace - Five	
Ace - Four	
Ace - Three	
Ace - Two	
Aces	

   b. If X is the total number of cards used and Y is the adjustment amount, what algebra statement represents Mike's pattern?

Card Tricks and Algebra

Here is an interesting card trick.

Step 1: Pick a card.

Step 2: Double the face value of the card (Aces = 1, Jacks = 11, Queens = 12, Kings = 13).

Step 3: Add 3 to your result.

Step 4: Multiply your last answer by 5.

Step 5: Add 1 to your result if your card is a Club. Add 2 to your result if your card is a Diamond. Add 3 to your result if your card is a Heart. Add 4 to your result if your card is a Spade.

What is your final result?

Step 6: To predict the card, subtract 15 from the final total. The right digit of the answer represents the suit of the card (1 = Club, 2 = Diamond, 3 = Heart, 4 = Spade). The left digit or digits is the number value of the card drawn. For example, if your result is 83, the card is the Eight of Hearts. If your result is 134, the card is the King of Spades.

Questions

Why does this trick work? Use algebra to explain your answer.

Pascal's Triangle Card Trick

Magicians often use mathematics in their tricks.

Suppose you are a spectator at a magic show where you are given a deck of cards with the Tens and face cards removed and the template below.

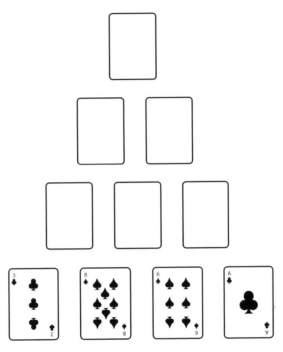

Imagine you were asked to place any 4 cards, face up, in the bottom row. The magician claims (s)he can predict the top card in the pyramid immediately. Is (s)he correct? Let's try an example. Suppose a 3, 8, 6 and 1 were dealt and the magician's step-by-step instructions were followed.

Step 1: Build each row above the base by using addition and "casting out nines." That is, if the sum is greater than 9, 9 is subtracted from the result to determine the card. For example, the first 2 cards in the bottom row of the diagram add to 11. Since 11 is not in the deck, 9 is subtracted. The new result is 2. So, you must put a two above the first pair of cards. The second and third cards add to 14, so a Five, or 14-9, is place above them. The third and fourth cards add to 7, so a Seven goes above them.

Step 2: Continue the procedure outlined in Step 1 until the pyramid reaches the top card, which is placed face down by the magician. When this card is turned over, it will be the correct value for the final sum.

Pascal's Triangle Card Trick

Questions

1. Bill said, "The magician's trick is related to one of the world's most famous number patterns called Pascal's triangle." He said that Pascal's triangle looks like this:

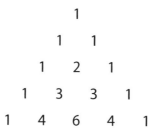

He also said that if you take the fourth row of the triangle (1, 3, 3, 1) and match it with the bottom row of the card trick you can find the top card by multiplying corresponding entries, adding the results and casting out nines on the answer. 1 x (3) + 3 x (8) + 3 x (6) + 1 x (1) = 46 or 1. Does it work? Show several examples.

2. Increase the number of cards in the initial or bottom of the pyramid to 5 and try the trick again. Does it still work?

3. Do you think the pyramid trick would work with any number of cards in the initial row? Explain.

4. Samantha said she could do the same pyramid card trick using all the cards in a deck if you just cast out thirteens rather than nines when the answers get too big. Is she correct? Explain.

5. Ed said he could prove the tricks work all the time by using algebra. Do you agree? Explain.

6. Make up your own pyramid card trick. Record your trick and answer.

Selected Answers and Comments

Page 6-10: Card Suit Race. The game board on page 7 is designed for a short game. Pages 8-10 can be used for a longer game by copying and taping the pages together to form a long track. For games involving basic facts, try taping one copy of page 7, multiple copies of page 8 and one copy of page 9 together to form a very long track.

Page 15: Cover All. There are many possible variations of this game. A few examples are to allow the use of addition and subtraction, allow the use of addition, subtraction, multiplication, and division or change the value of the cards so that the black cards are positive and the red cards are negative.

Pages 16-17: Decision Maker. This game can help students develop self-restraint. It may be helpful to demonstrate this game with a whole class divided into two teams the first time it is played with a group. Some teachers also find it effective to set up this game as a station activity for small groups.

Pages 28-29: Horseshoe Race. Some teachers enjoy creating a giant horseshoe game board for work with the entire class divided into two teams. Typically these giant horseshoes are ten pages long and five pages wide. They are created by duplicating several copies of page 19 and then trimming and taping the pages together to make the track. When a card or cards are drawn and the player/team has the correct color and gives a correct answer (s)he/they move forward that amount. For example, if the red team drew the Jack of Hearts and Three of Diamonds, and gave the correct sum (13), they would move ahead 13 spaces.

Pages 37-38: Let's Predict. This is an interesting strategy game where players/teams quickly learn the critical point in predicting. Skillful players will also learn to adjust their guesses based on the cards remaining in the pack. Increasing or decreasing the number of cards in the layout or by using subsets of the deck can also vary the game. For young children, using only Ace-Five or Ace-Ten may be important. Another variation some groups enjoy is having each player pay his/her opponent rather than the pack when (s)he is unable to make a correct prediction.

Page 45: Multiples of 7. Some students enjoy making this a competitive game by taking turns and then comparing scores to determine the winner of a game.

Pages 49-51: Pitch It. Note that copies of the target must be made to play the game. Also note that each target should be labeled with a value that is appropriate for the players. Some students may be initially frustrated by the difficulty of tossing a card so that it lands on a target. Providing them with 3 small boxes will reduce frustration. There are many more variations of this game. A few examples are shown. 1. Change the operation to addition, subtraction, multiplication or division. In subtraction games, start with a score of 200 and work toward 0. In division games, start with 6,000 and targets that are factors of 6,000, such as 2, 3 and 5. Low score wins. Calculators may be useful. 2. Change the values of the cards so that the black cards represent positive integers and the red cards represent negative integers. Then change the scoring rules so that players may win by scoring +200 or -200.

Pages 53-54: Quick Stop. Some players will need a record sheet to help organize their play. A format similar to page 17 may be useful.

Page 55-56: Ring Your Neck. This game is an interesting combination of skill and luck. Some students will develop a strategy for consistently getting the 50-point bones by working backwards. For example, in a 13-card game, a player can always get the final card by taking the cards in the positions that are circled. An example of the strategy for a 21-card game is also shown. Note that both examples show how transferring a real world problem into mathematical language makes the problem simpler!

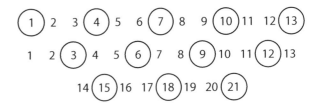

Selected Answers and Comments

When students play the 13 card games, it is useful to follow up the game with a discussion about the maximum and minimum scores possible in a game. For example, the maximum score possible for a multiplication game with 2 players and no bonus is 6,514,649,856. The minimum score for a division game with 2 players and no bonus is 1.535001914 E-4 or .00015350019414. Some students will also note that until addition and subtraction, having a bonus score is "no big deal" in multiplication and division games, but taking the last card is important because a player can increase or decrease his/her score significantly.

To make the standard game more challenging, change the rules so that the operation changes after each round. For example, round 1 is addition, round 2 is subtraction, round 3 is multiplication and round 4 is division. Rounds 5-8 could recycle the operations. Some groups also enjoy special values for cards such as One-eyed Jacks (100), the Queen of Spades (50), etc. Another variation that students enjoy is to award the 50-point bonus to the player/team that avoids taking the last card. Some classes call this variation the Poison Necklace Game.

Page 71: Creating Line Symmetry. Introduce the game by dividing the entire class into 2 teams and playing a demo game using cards on the overhead projector can be helpful. Some students may want to play or create a variation of the game. One example is shown.

Change the rules so that additional points are given if a player/team can use a card that has line symmetry (Note: If we ignore numerals and small suit marks, all the cards except the face cards have line symmetry).

Page 73: Let's Convert. The purpose of this game is to provide students with oral and written practice in converting measurements from one metric unit to another. The game assumes students have been introduced to the metric system, using a "hands on" approach.

Page 74-75: Let's Estimate. The purpose of this game is to provide students with practice estimating and measuring line segments. Note that students can also measure the segments in millimeters.

Page 81-82: Point Symmetry Rummy. Some students may improve their strategy by figuring out which cards in a 52-card deck possess rotational or point symmetry. Note that strategies will vary slightly based on the design of the deck used.

Page 88-90: Compare and Pair. Because of the similarities of the data analysis games, some teachers have their class work in groups and then assign one game to each group and have them share results for discussion. 1. A sample set of 10 games from a class is shown below. For this set of games, the mean score is 6.7, the mode is 2 and 14 and the median is 5.5.

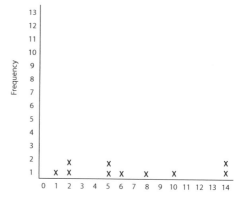

2. By matching or pairing it with another king.
3. No. The placeholder slots remain in the same positions, so 4 new cards are dealt and the game continues.
4. Answers will vary.
5. Sketches will vary. The range for the sample games in exercise 1 is 14. The standard deviation is 4.7387.
6. Yes. For the sample data above, <1%!
7. No. If a player can only win by getting a score of 0, (s)he does not have an equal chance of winning, so the game is not fair. However, the definition of winning could be adjusted, based on statistics, to make the game fair.
8. The major objective of *Compare and Pair* is data analysis. Some students may enjoy an extra challenge of collecting data on the results of increasing the number of piles in the line to 5, 6, 7, 8, 9, or 10 as a project. Some

Selected Answers and Comments

might also like to examine the results of decreasing the number of piles in the line to 2 or 3. Students should note that as the number of piles increases, the frequency of winning increases. If a class is studying fractions, decimals or percents, the data collected from the class can be a useful springboard for practice or review. A set of sample questions is shown below. How many games have been played? What percent of the games have been won? What fraction of the games had a result of 14 cards remaining?

Pages 93-94: Elevens. The purpose of this game is to provide a statistical experience involving finding the mean, median, mode and drawing a histogram picture of the data. If students have access to a graphing calculator, they can perform these tasks using technology. If a group or class plays 100 games, the results can be a useful springboard to or review of fractions, decimals and percent. When one class played 100 games, they won 72% of the time!

1. Then mean and median will vary, but the mode will be 0. Some teachers enjoy having all students in a class display their results using one large bar graph to dramatically show that the mode in this game is zero.
2. The game would be over because no 2 cards have a sum of eleven. The score would be 43.
3. 43.
4. Answers will vary. One question that quickly emerges is, "what is the win threshold?"
6. Yes. More than 50% of the games.
7. No, if we assume the charge for playing the game is $1 and the payoff for each game is $1. However, the house charge for playing the game and the payoff could be adjusted, based on statistics, to make the game fair.

Pages 95-99: Face Cards around the Perimeter. Having players tape together copies of pages 100 and 101 will help focus their attention and reduce confusion about where the cards should be played.

1. No. The Twos and Eights sum to ten, so they can be removed.
2. Answers will vary. Results from a set of 100 games are shown. Some students are surprised that 75% of the time the score is 9 or above.
Mode = 10, Median = 10, Q1 = 9, Q3 = 11, Mean = 9.65

3. The worst possible score is zero. This can happen in many ways. Four examples are shown.

4 Sixes, 4 Sevens, 4 Eights, 4 Nines

4 Sixes, 4 Sevens, 4 Eights, 3 Nines, 1 Five

4 Aces, 4 Twos, 4 Threes, 4 Fours

4 Aces, 4 Twos, 4 Threes, 3 Fours, 1 Five

Some talented students may enjoy comparing the results when the rules are changed so that the game ends when the array is filled and no cards can be removed, or when a face card is drawn and cannot be played.
4. Graphs will vary.
5. Answers will vary. Some students will comment on the lack of low scores such as 0, 1, 2.
6. Yes.
7. No. In a fair game against the house, a player would win 50% of the time.

Pages 100-101: Getting Even. 1. Below is a bar graph showing the results of 25 games from a class. Students should note that all results are even and be able to explain why this occurs. Many students will also note that an odd number + an odd number = an even number ($O + E = O$, $E + O = O$, and $E + E = E$). A few students will also note that $O - O = E$, $O - E = O$, $E - O = O$, $E - E = E$, and $O \times O = O$, $O \times E = E$, $E \times O = E$, $E \times E = E$.

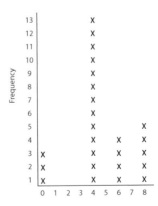

Number of Cards Remaining in the Line

Selected Answers and Comments

2. Yes. In the set of games above, the class won 3 out of 25, or 12% of the games.

3. Students should begin to formulate a strategy to win or at least achieve a low score. Typical responses involve comments such as, "fixing the ends and then play the middle." To a student this generally means setting up the 3 or 4 cards on each end of the line so that odds and evens correspond. This will ensure that the last set of 6-8 cards that are removed are even.

Page 102: Lucky Number. Some teachers enjoy having all students in a class display their results side by side, using one large bar graph. Others aggregate the data.

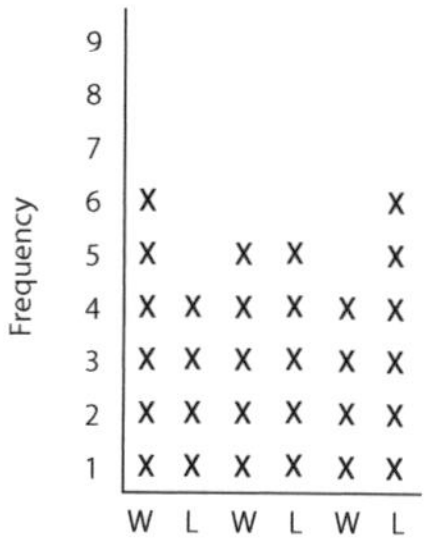

```
        9
        8
        7
   F    6  X              X
   r    5  X     X  X     X
   e    4  X  X  X  X  X  X
   q    3  X  X  X  X  X  X
   u    2  X  X  X  X  X  X
   e    1  X  X  X  X  X  X
   n       W  L  W  L  W  L
   c
   y
```

Follow Up Questions:
1. What patterns do you notice in the results? Explain your observations.
2. Is it possible to win this game? If so, how often does it occur?
3. Suppose you compared the results of a set of games using the cards Ace through Eight of a deck with the results of the same number of games using the Sixes through Kings. Do you think the results would be the same?

Pages 103-104: Matched Pair. Matched Pair leaves you mostly at the mercy of the shuffle. There is almost no opportunity for strategy, but wins are fairly common. A sample graph of 25 games is shown below.

Players should note that the results are always an even number. This is because we start with an even number of cards (32) and remove cards of the same rank in pairs.

Variation 1: Theoretically, the results of games using a comparable number of different cards should be the same.

Variation 2: Keeping the number of cards the same, 32 total, Aces through Eight, and decreasing the number of piles to 4 decreases the chance of winning.

Variation 3: Some students may enjoy an extra challenge of collecting data on the results of increasing the number of piles in the circle to 9, using Ace through Nine, with 4 cards in each pile, or ten, using Ace through Ten, with 4 cards in each pile. If you are studying fractions, decimals, percent or basic ideas from statistics, the data collected from a class can be a useful springboard to a discussion. A set of sample questions are shown below.

> How many games have been played?
> What percent of the games have been won?
> What fraction of the games have been lost?

Page 108: Find the Joker. Young players may need to play the game using left, right, up or down clues. They may also find it helpful to have a copy of the instructions or a directional compass for reference as they play.

Page 110-111: Power Play. Suggested follow up questions are provided below.

What is the largest core possible in single round of a game of Power Play if 2 ordinary dice are used to play the game? Answer: $6^6 = 46656$.

> What is the smallest score possible in a single round of a game of Power Play if 2 ordinary dice are used to play the game? Answer: One to any power. $1^6 = 1$.

> What is the second largest score possible in a single round of a game of Power Play if 2 ordinary dice are used to play the game? Answer: $5^6 = 15625$.

> What is the second smallest score possible in a single round of a game of Power Play if 2 ordinary dice are used to play the game? Answer: $2^1 = 2$.

Selected Answers and Comments

What is the highest total score possible in an 8-round game of Power Play using two ordinary dice? Answer: 46656 x 8 = 373248.

Page 116: Card Pick Up Games. There are many variations of this game. For example: Place 11, 12 or 13 cards on the table as shown in the Rules and Play. Each player is allowed to take 1, 2 or 3 cards at a time. The player who takes the last card wins. Place 11, 12 or 13 cards on the table as shown in the Rules and Play. Each player is allowed to take 1, 2 or 3 cards at a time. The player who takes the last card loses. Students should select one of the games and analyze who wins carefully, so that they can answer the following question. If 2 people play the game and both are very skillful, who should win? Explain your answer. The key to the solution is using the problem solving strategy of working backwards.

Page 121-122: Street Hustler. This is an old game that has many names, 3-Card Monty, Location-Location-Location, Position-Position-Position, etc. The game has been used by con artists to bilk unsuspecting players by allowing them to win when the games involves small bets and then making a sting on larger bets. Some stings are set up by using a partner who artificially raises the betting level. For example, the dealer says, "Who wants to play?" When a customer expresses interest, (s)he responds with the comment, "How much are you willing to bet?" If the potential customer responds with a small amount, such as $1, the partner in crime, who pretends to be a potential player, says a higher amount, such as $10, in an attempt to set up a bid to play war. If the partner wins the bid to play war, (s)he is allowed to win in order to set the bait for the next game with the unsuspecting victim. Typical strategies identified by students are watching carefully and selecting the same position. Some students might also want to use statistics to explore the question; Do players pick the middle card more frequently?

Page 123: Two Aces and a Deuce. After playing several games, ask students to describe their strategy. Some students may confess that they peek! Others will use reasoning. One student explanation is provided below.

> Case 1: One player has a deuce. "If I get the Deuce card, I know my opponent must have an Ace because there is only one Deuce."

> Case 2: Both players have an Ace. "If my opponent does not speak up immediately, (s)he must have an Ace. This only works as long as my opponent doesn't catch on!"

Students will discover that indirect proof is the best method of playing the game, even if they do not know what it is called. You may find it helpful to label this idea for them.

Page 124: Yes, No, You Got It!. The strategy used in this game has many practical applications. It is called a binary search technique and is frequently used by computer programmers to quickly locate specific items in sorted lists. Examples include locating phone numbers (directory assistance) and computer spell check programs. 1. 1 2. 4 3. You could ask card by card. There are 52 cards in the deck

Some students will enjoy playing additional variations of this game. A few examples are provided below.

> Change the value of the cards so that each black card is a positive integer and each red card is negative integer.

> Adjust the scoring scheme so that the player/team receives a score equal to the number of guesses required to identify the card. The player/team with the lowest total score at the end of the game wins.

Selected Answers and Comments

Pages 128-130: Fractions and Decimals In Between. Some students may need to play a whole numbers version of this game before working with fractions and decimals. To make the standard whole numbers game more challenging, change the rules so that a player/team must get 2 or 3 cards in between the initial pair that are drawn. For example, if a Two and King were drawn, then the player must draw two cards that have a value between 2 and 13.

Pages 133-134: Relay The Message. This is a game for the whole class, organized by rows, tables or teams. The purpose of the game is to review finding the percent of a number and to suggest non-traditional career options for women in science. Some students may also wish to create their own relay with a non-traditional vocation message. Be sure to review student creations carefully to avoid any surprise occupations that may be found inappropriate.

Pages 136-138: Tour the Planets. The first letter of each planet name is provided on the game board to help players remember the names of the planets. The full names for each planet, arranged in order according to their distance form the sun are: Mercury, Venus, Earth, Mars, Jupiter, Saturn, Uranus, Neptune, Pluto. The hints can be removed from the game board after a few games. Some students find a helpful key word for remembering the 3 planets between Jupiter and Pluto is the word SUN.

Pages 139-141: Tour The USA. Below is a list of all 50 states and their capitals.

Alabama	Montgomery
Alaska	Juneau
Arizona	Phoenix
Arkansas	Little Rock
California	Sacramento
Colorado	Denver
Connecticut	Hartford
Delaware	Dover
Florida	Tallahassee
Georgia	Atlanta
Hawaii	Honolulu
Idaho	Boise
Illinois	Springfield
Indiana	Indianapolis
Iowa	Des Moines
Kansas	Topeka
Kentucky	Frankfort
Louisiana	Baton Rouge
Maine	Augusta
Maryland	Annapolis
Massachusetts	Boston
Michigan	Lansing
Minnesota	St. Paul
Mississippi	Jackson
Missouri	Jefferson City
Montana	Helena
Nebraska	Lincoln
Nevada	Carson City
New Hampshire	Concord
New Jersey	Trenton
New Mexico	Santa Fe
New York	Albany
North Carolina	Raleigh
North Dakota	Bismarck
Ohio	Columbus
Oklahoma	Oklahoma City
Oregon	Salem
Pennsylvania	Harrisburg
Rhode Island	Providence
South Carolina	Columbia
South Dakota	Pierre
Tennessee	Nashville

Selected Answers and Comments

Texas	Austin
Utah	Salt Lake City
Vermont	Montpelier
Virginia	Richmond
Washington	Olympia
West Virginia	Charleston
Wisconsin	Madison
Wyoming	Cheyenne

Page 142: Card Patterns. 1. Nine of Clubs, Jack of Clubs, King of Clubs.
2. Jack of Spades.
3. The suit pattern is Clubs, Diamonds, Hearts, Spades. The numbers increase by one. The cards are Seven of Hearts, Eight of Spades, Nine of Clubs, and Ten of Diamonds.
4. The pattern is black, black, red, red with cards in the odd positions increasing by 1 and cards in the even numbered positions have a number value of 1 (2, 1, 3, 1, 4, 1, 5, 1, 6). The mystery cards are the Ace of Spades, red Five, Ace of Diamonds, black Six.

Page 143-144: Consecutive Numbers Card Puzzles.

1. Answers will vary. One example is shown.

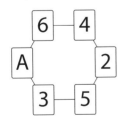

2. Answers will vary. One example is shown.

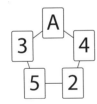

3. Answers will vary. One example is shown.

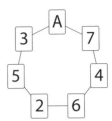

4. Answers will vary. One example is shown.

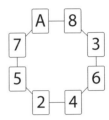

5. Answers will vary. One example is shown.

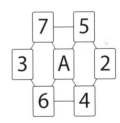

6. Answers will vary. One example is shown.

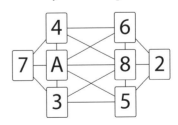

Selected Answers and Comments

7. Answers will vary. One example is shown.

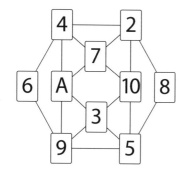

8. Answers will vary. One example is shown.

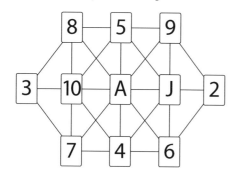

9. Answers will vary. One example is shown.

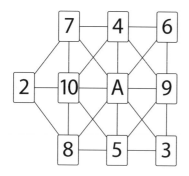

10. Answers will vary. One example is shown.

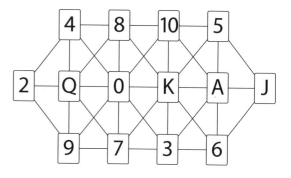

Pages 145-146: Finding Sums. Many students find it interesting to create and solve puzzles using the templates in this activity. For example, one student modified problem 4 as follows: Use one complete suit and a Joker. Place the value of cards on the diagram so that the sum of each line is 18. Note: Joker = 0.

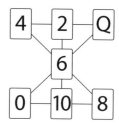

1. Answers will vary. One example is shown.

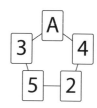

2. Answers will vary. One example is shown.

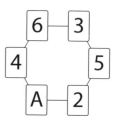

Selected Answers and Comments

3. Answers will vary. One example is shown.

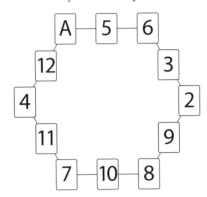

4. Answers will vary. One example is shown.

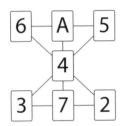

5. Answers will vary. One example is shown.

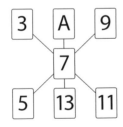

6. Answers will vary. One example is shown.

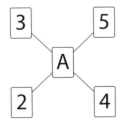

7. Answers will vary. One example is shown.

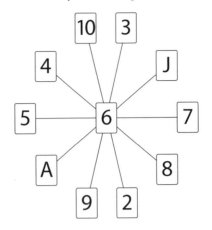

Page 147-148: More Finding Sums.

1.

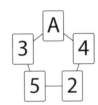

2. Answers will vary.

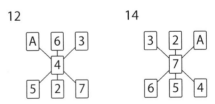

Selected Answers and Comments

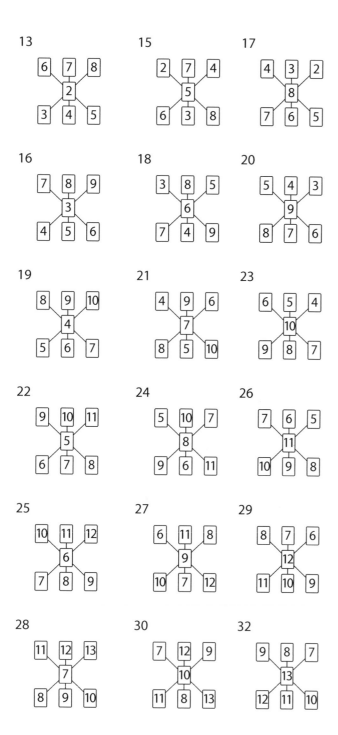

13

6	7	8
2		
3	4	5

15

2	7	4
5		
6	3	8

17

4	3	2
8		
7	6	5

16

7	8	9
3		
4	5	6

18

3	8	5
6		
7	4	9

20

5	4	3
9		
8	7	6

19

8	9	10
4		
5	6	7

21

4	9	6
7		
8	5	10

23

6	5	4
10		
9	8	7

22

9	10	11
5		
6	7	8

24

5	10	7
8		
9	6	11

26

7	6	5
11		
10	9	8

25

10	11	12
6		
7	8	9

27

6	11	8
9		
10	7	12

29

8	7	6
12		
11	10	9

28

11	12	13
7		
8	9	10

30

7	12	9
10		
11	8	13

32

9	8	7
13		
12	11	10

Page 149: Five-Pointed Star. 1. Answers will vary. Accept all answers. Emphasize finding as many solutions as possible.

2.

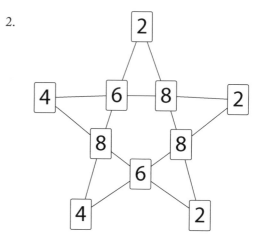

3. No. Four. Many students enjoy creating and sharing their puzzles. One sample student creation and solution is shown. Use 2 Tens, 4 Sixes, and 4 Fours. Place the cards on the star so that the sum of each line is 24.

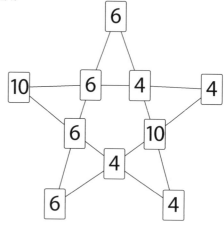

Selected Answers and Comments

Page 150: Six-Pointed Star.

1.

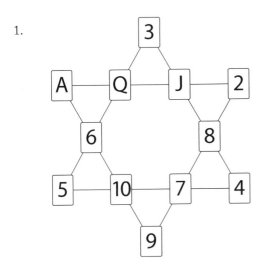

2. The sum is 30.
3.

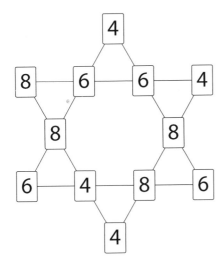

Pages 151-152: Bullseye. Many teachers use this activity as a part of teaching students mental arithmetic. The power of the Bullseye is the generic format. By eliminating the cards and creating an open-ended master, students and teachers can create practice and maintenance on a variety of math topics such as addition, subtraction, multiplication and division of whole numbers, fractions, decimals, integers, etc. If students create a Bullseye grid assignment, their efforts can be used as class starters and fillers.

Pages 153: Operation Table Puzzles.

+	A♠	6♦
9♣	10	15
7♣	8	13

x	6♦	3♠
8♦	48	24
9♣	54	27

-	9♣	5♠
K♠	4	8
J♥	2	6

x	10♠	3♦
10♥	100	30
7♣	70	21

-	7♠	8♣
J♥	4	3
10♥	3	2

+	8♣	9♠
9♠	17	18
Q♦	20	21

-	2♠	8♦
9♥	7	A
Q♥	10	4

+	8♣	A♥
5♦	13	6
K♣	21	14

x	8♦	7♦
9♣	72	63
4♣	32	28

Some students may enjoy the challenge of creating a puzzle involving division. A sample creation is shown below.

÷		A♦
Q♣		
	3	

Selected Answers and Comments

Pages 153: *Guess My Rule.*

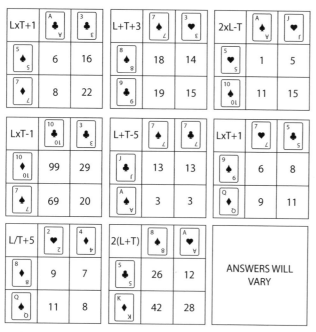

Using a deck to have students draw a card and guess easier rules, such as doubling the value of a single card, is an effective way to introduce this activity. Some students may enjoy the challenge of creating a puzzle with more than one answer for a cell. A sample creation is shown below.

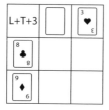

Classes may also enjoy reviewing this notion of making up your own operation and symbol on or before holidays or special events such as Halloween.

Page 155: Border Patrol Card Puzzles.
The problem solving strategy encouraged by this series of puzzles is working backwards. A timer may be useful for this activity.

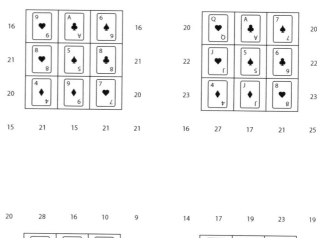

Page 156: More Border Patrol Card Puzzles.
The problem solving strategies encouraged by this series of puzzles are working backwards and systematic trial and error. A timer may be useful for this activity.

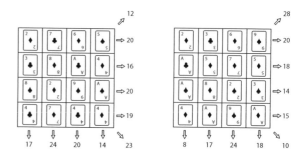

3. Answers will vary.

Selected Answers and Comments

Pages 157-158: Cards, Triangles and Patterns Card Puzzles. Encourage students to use the T, R and L algebraic notation to describe their rules.
2. Prediction: 10. Rule = Top x Left x Right.
3. Prediction: 9. Rule = Top x Left – Right.
4. Prediction: 48. Rule = T(L + R).
5. Prediction: 0. Rule = T(R – L).
6. Prediction: 4. Rule = T/(R/L).

Page 159-160: Nine Card Logic Puzzles. Answers will vary. One example is shown.

For an additional challenge, add the restrictions that the product of the cards in column 1 must be 20, the product of the cards in column 2 must be 9, and the product of the cards in column 3 must be 16. Some students will also enjoy making up their own puzzle.

Pages 164-166: Logic Puzzles.
1. 3 Fives
2. 2 Fives, 2 Aces and 1 Three
3. 1 Five, 3 Threes and 2 Aces
4. 1 Five, 1 Three and 2 Aces
5. Impossible. The sum of 3 odd numbers is an odd number.

6. Arrangements will vary. One example is shown below.

7. Answers will vary.

Pages 167-168: Windmill Card Puzzles.
1. Four of a kind. All sums are even.
2. 2 Aces and 2 Twos or, if jokers are allowed, 2 Jokers and 2 Threes.
3. 2 Sevens and 2 Sixes, 2 Eights and 2 Fives, 2 Nines and 2 Fours, 2 Tens and 2 Threes, 2 Jacks and 2 Twos, 2 Queens and 2 Aces, and if Jokers are allowed, 2 Kings and 2 Jokers.
4. 1 Ace and 2 Fives placed as shown.

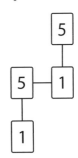

5. An Eight and any pair placed as shown.

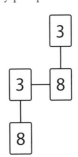

Selected Answers and Comments

6. Two Kings and two Tens.
7. Two Nines placed as shown and any other pair.

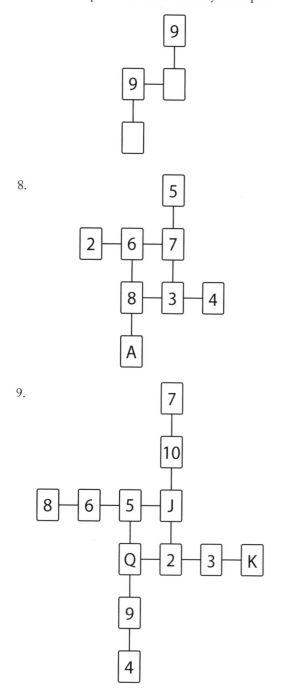

8.

9.

10. Answers will vary. Some students may inadvertently create problems that are impossible. For example, using the cards Ace through Queen and the diagram for problem 9. Accept all creations!

Page 169: Take a Walk.
1a. 8 ⇨ 9 ⇨ 7 ⇨ 8 ⇨ 5 = 37
1b. 8 ⇨ 6 ⇨ 5 ⇨ 8 ⇨ 5 = 32
1c. Yes, several. For example, 35, 36, 37.
2a. 8 ⇨ 9 ⇨ 5 ⇨ 6 ⇨ 9 ⇨ 8 ⇨ 5 = 50
2b. 8 ⇨ 6 ⇨ 5 ⇨ 9 ⇨ 7 ⇨ 8 ⇨ 5 = 48
2c. Yes. 48
3. 5 cards:
3a. 8 ⇨ 9 ⇨ 7 ⇨ 8 ⇨ 5 = 20160
3b. 8 ⇨ 6 ⇨ 5 ⇨ 8 ⇨ 5 = 604800
3c. Yes, for example, 20160. 7 cards:
3a. 8 ⇨ 9 ⇨ 5 ⇨ 6 ⇨ 9 ⇨ 8 ⇨ 5 = 777600
3b. 8 ⇨ 6 ⇨ 5 ⇨ 9 ⇨ 7 ⇨ 8 ⇨ 5 = 604800
3c. Yes, a and b are examples.
4. 5 cards:
4a. -8 ⇨ -6 ⇨ 9 ⇨ 8 ⇨ 5 = 8
4b. -8 ⇨ -9 ⇨ -7 ⇨ 8 ⇨ 5 = -11
4c. Yes, for example 8, -11. 7 cards:
4a. -8 ⇨ -6 ⇨ 9 ⇨ 8 ⇨ 5 ⇨ 8 ⇨ 5 = 21
4b. -8 ⇨ -6 ⇨ 5 ⇨ 9 ⇨ -7 ⇨ 8 ⇨ 5 = -12
4c. Yes, 21, -12. Pre-Algebra students may enjoy this calculator challenge: Find the answer to problem 3 if the red cards are negative and the black cards are positive.
5. 10

Page 170: Spider Math.
1a. 9 ⇨ 9 ⇨ 8 ⇨ 7 ⇨ 5 = 38
1b. 2 ⇨ 4 ⇨ 4 ⇨ 5 ⇨ 3 = 18 1c. Yes, although every path can be reversed.
2a. 9 ⇨ 9 ⇨ 8 ⇨ 7 = 33
2b. 6 ⇨ 3 ⇨ 6 ⇨ 2 = 17
2c. Yes, for example, 33 and 17.
3. Start anywhere and collect 5 cards.
3a. 9 ⇨ 9 ⇨ 8 ⇨ 7 ⇨ 5 = 22680
3b. 6 ⇨ 3 ⇨ 6 ⇨ 2 = 216
3c. Yes, although every path can be reversed. Start at a corner and collect 4 cards.
3a. 9 ⇨ 9 ⇨ 8 ⇨ 7 = 4536
3b. 6 ⇨ 3 ⇨ 6 ⇨ 2 = 216
3c. Yes, a and b are examples.

Selected Answers and Comments

4. Start anywhere and collect 5 cards 4a. 8 ⇨ 5 ⇨ 3 ⇨ 8
⇨ 5 = 29
4b. -9 ⇨ -4 ⇨ -2 ⇨ -6 ⇨ 3 = 18
4c. Yes, although any path can be reversed. Start at a corner and collect 4 cards.
4a. 8 ⇨ 5 ⇨ 4 ⇨ -2 = 15
4b. -7 ⇨ 8 ⇨ -9 ⇨ -4 = -12
4c. Yes, a and b are examples.
Pre-algebra students may enjoy this calculator challenge: Find the answer to problem 3, if the red cards are negative and the black cards are positive.

Page 171: Fancy Footwork Featuring Fours Card Puzzles.

0. $(4 - 4) + (4 - 4)$
1. $(4 + 4) / (4 + 4)$
2. $4 / 4 + 4 / 4$
3. $4 - (4^{4 - 4})$
4. $4 \times (4^{4 - 4})$
6. $(4 + 4) / 4 + 4$
7. $44 / 4 - 4$
8. $4 \times 4 - 4 - 4$
9. $4 / 4 + 4 + 4$
10. $(44 - 4) / 4$
11. $44 / (\sqrt{4}\sqrt{4})$
12. $(4 + 44) / 4$
13. $44 / 4 + \sqrt{4}$
14. $\sqrt{4}(4 + 4) - \sqrt{4}$
15. $44 / 4 + 4$
16. $4 \times 4 - 4 + 4$
17. $4 \times 4 + 4 / 4$
18. $\sqrt{4}(4 + 4) + \sqrt{4}$
19. $4! - 4 - 4 / 4$
20. $4(4 / 4 + 4)$
21. $(44 - \sqrt{4}) / \sqrt{4}$
22. $(44 \times \sqrt{4}) / 4$
23. $(44 + \sqrt{4}) / \sqrt{4}$
24. $4 \times 4 + 4 + 4$
25. $4! + (4^{4 - 4})$

26. $44 / \sqrt{4} + 4$
27. $4! + 4 - (4 / 4)$
28. $4(4 + 4) - 4$
29. $4! + 4 + 4 / 4$
30. $4(4 + 4) - \sqrt{4}$
31. $4! + (4 + 4!) / 4$
32. $\sqrt{4}(4 + 4) (\sqrt{4})$
33. $4! + (4 + (\sqrt{4} / .4))$
34. $4(4 + 4) + \sqrt{4}$
35. $4! + 44 / 4$
36. $4(4 + 4) + 4$
37. $((\sqrt{4} + 4!) / \sqrt{4}) + 4!$
    or $(4! + .4) / .4 - 4!$
38. $44 - 4 - \sqrt{4}$
39. $44 - (\sqrt{4} / .4)$ or $(4! / 4) / .4 + 4!$
40. $(44 - \sqrt{4} - \sqrt{4})$
41. $4(4^{(4 - 4)})$ or $\sin^{-1}({}^4\sqrt{4} / \sqrt{4}) - 4$
42. $44 - 4 + \sqrt{4}$
43. $44 - 4 / 4$ or $(\sqrt{4})(4!) - (\sqrt{4} / .4)$
44. $44 / 4 \times 4$
45. $44 + 4 / 4$
46. $(4! + 4!) - (4 / \sqrt{4})$ or $44 + 4 - \sqrt{4}$
47. $4! + 4! - 4 / 4$ or $4((4 + 4!) / 4)$
48. $4(4 + 4 + 4)$
    or $((\sqrt{4} / 4\%) - (4 / \sqrt{4}))$
49. $4! + 4! + (4 / 4)$ or $44 + (\sqrt{4} / .4)$
50. $44 + 4 + \sqrt{4}$ or $(\sqrt{4} / 4\%)(4 / 4)$

Students enjoy trying to create all the numbers from 1-100, 101-200, 201-1000, the current year, their birth year, etc. for additional challenges. A bulletin board showing answers and progress toward a class goal can be useful. Similar challenges can be provided with other sets of four cards. For example, Fancy Footwork can feature Fives, Sixes, Sevens, etc.

Page 172: Shifting Cards Puzzles.
1. Answers will vary. One example is shown.

2. Answers will vary. One example is shown.

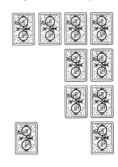

Pages 173-174: Switching Cards Puzzles.
Ace=1, Jack=11, Queen=12, King=13.

2.

Number of Cards	4	5	6	7	8	9	10	11	12	13
Number of Cards	4	4	4	8	10	15	17	24	35	36

Selected Answers and Comments

Page 175: Magic Square Card Puzzle. Arrangements will vary. Examples are shown below.

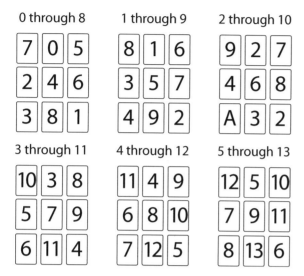

0 through 8

7	0	5
2	4	6
3	8	1

1 through 9

8	1	6
3	5	7
4	9	2

2 through 10

9	2	7
4	6	8
A	3	2

3 through 11

10	3	8
5	7	9
6	11	4

4 through 12

11	4	9
6	8	10
7	12	5

5 through 13

12	5	10
7	9	11
8	13	6

Some students may also enjoy the additional challenge of solving 4 x 4 magic square card puzzles. Two sample challenges are provided. Use 4 Aces, 4 Nines, 4 Fives and 4 Kings. Place the cards in a 4 x 4 array so that the sum of each row, column and diagonal is 28.

1	5	13	9
9	13	5	1
5	1	9	13
13	9	1	5

Use the cards that are multiples of 2. Place the cards in a 4 x 4 array so that the sum of each row, column and diagonal is 30.

6	4	12	8
8	12	4	6
4	6	8	12
12	8	6	4

Page 176: Circles and Reasoning Card Puzzle. One effective way to introduce this set of puzzles is to use hula hoops, yarn or string and actual cards.

Page 177: Circles and Reasoning Card Puzzle II. Answers will vary. Any 2 sets of three of a kind, placed as shown below, will work.

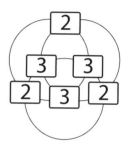

Page 178: Circles and Reasoning Card Puzzle III. Four Aces or two Jokers plus a pair of other cards.

Page 179: Circles and Reasoning Card Puzzle IV. Initially many students will think this is impossible, but it can be done if Jokers are used in the center cells and four of a kind are placed in the remaining cells.

Page 180: Olympic Rings Card Puzzle. Answers will vary. One example is shown below.

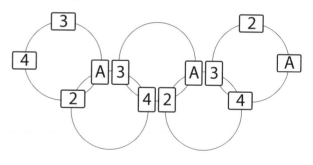

Page 181: Secret Messages.
1. No Big Deal.
3. Answers will vary, a few examples are shown.

Know when to hold 'em
It's a good deal
Cut your losses

Selected Answers and Comments

You're bluffing
Ante up
House of cards
Busted
Odds are against it
No limit
You hit the jackpot

Page 182: Check Out The Symbols.
1. Aces = 3, Face Cards = 4, All other cards = value + 2. So we get 3 x 4, plus 4 x 12, plus sum of the values of a suit added to the corner adjustment for each card in each suit.

Aces: 3 x 4 = 12
Face Cards: 4 x 12 = 48
Others: 4 x 72 = 288
Total: 348

2. Face cards have 4 symbols, Deuces have 4 symbols, and Aces have 3 symbols. So, 52 − 20 = 32. 3. The Aces have 3 symbols. So, 4/52 or 1/13. 4. The face cards and Deuces have 4 symbols. So, 16/52 or about 31%.

Page 183: Place Value. 1. There are four possibilities. 418, 172, 254, 336. 2. 6216 3. 96349 4. Answers will vary. Samples are shown.

Use the cards Ace through Nine of a suit. Find the cards and five-digit number. All five digits are the same. The sum of all the digits is 20. Answer: 44444.

Use the cards Ace through Nine of a suit. Find the cards and five-digit number. The first two digits are the same. The two digits are the same. The hundreds digit is a one. The sum of all the digits is 29. Answer: 55199.

Use the cards Ace through Nine of a suit. Find the cards and five-digit number. The ten thousands digit is one-fourth the thousands digit. The hundreds digit is one-half the thousands digit. The tens digit

is the sum of the ones and hundreds digit. The ones digit is a three. The sum of all the digits is 15. Answer: 14253.

Use the Joker and Ace through Nine of a suit. Find the cards and five-digit number. One of the digits is a zero. Four of the digits are the same. The thousands digit is nil. The sum of the digits is 36. Answer: 90999.

Use the cards Ace through Nine of a suit. Find the cards and five-digit number. The ten thousands digit is half the one digit. The thousands digit is three-fourths of the ten thousands digit. The hundreds digit is the sum of the ten and one thousands digit. The ten digit is half the ones digit. The sum of all five digits is 26. Answer: 43748.

Page 184-187: Dissecting A Card. 2a. Isosceles Right Triangle 2b. Isosceles Right Triangle 2c. Isosceles Right Triangle 2d. Isosceles Right Triangle 2e. Isosceles Right Triangle 2f. Parallelogram 2g. Square 2h. Rectangle 2i. Isosceles Triangle 2j. Isosceles Triangle 2k. Isosceles Triangle 2l. Isosceles Triangle 2m. Rectangle. 3. Perimeter ≈ 42.8cm, Area = 114.49 cm^2 4. Perimeter ≈ 36.2 cm, Area = 28.09 cm^2 5. Perimeter ≈ 60.8 cm, Area = 231.04 cm^2, Sketches will vary, one example is shown.

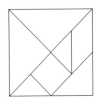

6. A = 57.245 cm^2, B = 57.245 cm^2, C = 14.045 cm^2, D = 14.045 cm^2, E = 28.125 cm^2, F = 28.55 cm^2, G = 28.09 cm^2, H = 19.8 cm^2, I = 4.95 cm^2, J = 4.95 cm^2, K = 5.7 cm^2, L = 5.7 cm^2, M = 45.6 cm^2

Selected Answers and Comments

Piece	Fraction of Whole	Percent of Whole
A	57.245/322.24	17.76%
B	57.245/322.24	17.76%
C	14.045/322.24	4.36%
D	14.045/322.24	4.36%
E	28.125/322.24	8.73%
F	28.55/322.24	8.86%
G	28.09/322.24	8.72%
H	19.8/322.24	6.14%
I	4.95/322.24	1.54%
J	4.95/322.24	1.54%
K	5.7/322.24	1.77%
L	5.7/322.24	1.77%
M	45.6/322.24	14.15%

After students have computed the percent each piece is of the whole card, have them find the sum of percentages (97.46%) and explain why it is not 100%. Some students may enjoy an extra credit challenge of making their own card dissection puzzle. You may want to limit the maximum number of pieces for this extra credit fun.

A logical link to a multicultural activity can be made by having students examine exercise 5 where they are asked to use the pieces labeled A, B, C, D, E, F and G to form a square. This is the famous, old Chinese Tangram. No one knows exactly when this problem made its first appearance, but scholars have found it in Chinese books published in 1803. They believe it was invented before that time and then spread westward to Europe and the United States. Another possible solution to the Tangram square problem is shown here. There are many more.

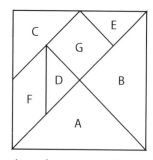

Another puzzle students enjoy solving with the 7 Tangram pieces is to make the cat below. As always, they also enjoy making up their own puzzles for their friends and family. Tangram Purists insist that all 7 pieces must be used in any puzzle and that no 2 pieces may overlap. Enjoy the fun and encourage them to visit the library to find out more about Tangrams.

Page 188-189: An Amazing 3-Stack Card Trick. This is a fascinating problem for a class project. Encourage the members of the class to make and share notes. A sample set of notes from a class is shown here.

We think the 3 stack sum + 10 = 13 + 13 + 13 + 13 = 52, but we're not sure. If we let S = "counting stack sum," A = value of the first card in one pile, B = value of the first card in a second pile, and C = value of the top card of unknown pile (or the card we are trying to predict). Then S + A + B + C = 52 or S − 3 + A + 1 + B + 1 + C + 1 = 52. By solving for C, we get C = 52 − (S-3) − (A+B).

First Card	1	2	3	4	5	6	7	8	9	10	11 Jack	12 Queen	13 King
Number in Pile	13 14-1	12 14-2	11 14-3	10 14-4	9 14-5	8 14-6	7 14-7	6 14-8	5 14-9	4 14-10	3 14-11	2 14-12	1 14-13

Here are some other things we found.

> *The 2 Stack Trick*: Deal the cards as in the 3-stack trick. Then select 2 piles. Turn one over. The answer will be the remainder if you count into the pack the stack sum + 24(11 + 13). 24 + A + B = 52. 52 − (S − 2) − 13 − A = B.

> We're trying to make a 4, 5 or 6 stack trick. No luck so far, but we wonder if they involve 9, 8, etc.?

Selected Answers and Comments

Page 190: Card Tricks and Algebra.

Step 1: Call the selected card x.
Step 2: Doubling the value, we get 2x.
Step 3: Adding 3, we get $2x + 3$.
Step 4: Multiply by 5 and we get $10x + 15$.
Step 5: Adding 1, 2, 3, or 4 we get $10x + 16$ (for Clubs), $10x + 17$ (for Diamonds), $10x + 18$ (for Hearts), $10x + 19$ (for Spades).
Step 6: Subtracting 15, we get $10x + 1$ (for Clubs), $10x + 2$ (for Diamonds), $10x + 3$ (for Hearts), $10x + 4$ (for Spades). So, the left digit, or digits, will be the number value of the card drawn and the right digit will be suit of the card.

Some students will enjoy the challenge of making up their own card trick.

Page 191-192: Pascal's Triangle Card Trick. 1. Yes. Examples will vary. 2. Yes. For example, if you start with a 9, 7, A, 5, 8 and use the numbers in the 5th row of the triangle you get: $1(9) + 4(7) + 6(1) + 4(5) + 1(8) = 71$. Processing this answer using casting out nines, we get 8. 3. Yes, within the limit of the cards available. Since only 36 cards are used, because tens and face cards are removed, the maximum number of cards in the base of the pyramid is 8. 4. Samantha is correct, if Jack = 11, Queen = 12, and King = 13. For example, start with a four-card base such as 3, 8, 6, A and the apex card will be 7. Using casting out thirteen's we get $46/13 = 3$ with a remainder of 7! Similarly, if you start with a five card base such as 9, 7, A, 5, 8, the apex card will be 6. Using casting out thirteen's we get $71/13 = 5$ with a remainder of 6! 5. Suppose we use the example as a sample. We can describe the general case of the pyramid with a four-card base as shown. Note that $C_1, C_2, C_3, \ldots C_{10}$ represent cards from the deck.

$$C_{10}$$
$$C_8 \quad C_9$$
$$C_5 \quad C_6 \quad C_7$$
$$C_1 \quad C_2 \quad C_3 \quad C_4$$

There are many ways to show the sum of $C_1 + C_2$, $C_2 + C_3$, etc. One convenient way to show the of $C_1 + C_2 = C_5$ is $C_5 = 9m + x$, where m is the integer part of the quotient $(C_1 + C_2)/9$ and the x is the remainder. In a similar manner, $C_6 = 9n + y$, where n is the integer part of the quotient $(C_2 + C_3)/9$ and y is the remainder. $C_7 = 9o + z$, where o is the integer part of the quotient $(C_3 + C_4)/9$ and z is the remainder.

Continuing, we get: $C_8 = C_5 + C_6$ or $C_8 = (9m + x) + (9n + y)$, $C_9 = C_6 + C_7$ or $C_9 = (9n + y) + (9o + z)$, $C_{10} = C_8 + C_9$ or $C_{10} = [(9m + x) + (9n + y)] + [(9n + y) + (9o + z)]$

Since 9m, 9n, and 9o are divisible by 9, the apex card must be the sum of the remainders or $x + 2y + z$. For example, if the base cards are 3, 8, 6, 1, then $x = 2$, $y = 5$, and $z = 7$. So, substituting we get $2 + 2(5) + 7 = 19$ or 1. Another way to look at this is to answer this question. If C_n is the apex card, is C_n = sum of the bottom row − 9 times the integer part of the Pascal adjustment? Looking at the case of computing C_{10} we get, $C_{10} = [(1C_1 + 3C_2 + 3C_3 + 1C_4) - (9 (\text{int } (1C_1 + 3C_2 + 3C_3 + 1C_4)/9))]$

For the base cards 3, 8, 6, 1, we get $46 - 45 = 1$.

6. Blaise Pascal was a French mathematician who lived in the 17th century. He made many interesting and useful discoveries in math and science. The triangle is named in the honor of this pioneer in the field of probability. The triangle has many uses in addition to this card trick. There are many useful references on Pascal's work that students might find of interest in most libraries. Two examples are Irving Adler's, *Giant Golden Book of Mathematics* and *Life Science Library Volume on Mathematics*. Some students may note that it is not always possible to build the pyramid with one deck of cards. For example, if the base of the pyramid is 3, 6, 9, 7, 6 you will run out of Sixes. Similarly, if you start with 9, 8, 1, 7, 4 you will run out of Eights.

Math in the Cards
© IPMG Publishing

Made in the USA
Columbia, SC
28 February 2020

88511168R00122